Journeys by Heart

RITA NAKASHIMA BROCK

Journeys by Heart

A Christology of Erotic Power

CROSSROAD · NEW YORK

1996

The Crossroad Publishing Company
370 Lexington Avenue, New York, NY 10017

Printed in the United States of America

Library of Congress Cataloging-in-Publication Data

Brock, Rita Nakashima
    Journeys by heart: a Christology of erotic power / Rita Nakashima
Brock.
        p.   cm.
    Bibliography: p.
    Includes index.
    ISBN 0-8245-1082-8 (pbk)
    1. Jesus Christ—Person and offices. 2. Feminist theology.
3. Bible. N. T. Mark—Criticism, interpretation, etc. I. Title.
BT205.B824 1988
232—dc19   88-25628
                                                                CIP

To Willis W. Fisher who showed me that
personal experience is the route
to our knowledge of truth and justice
and who taught me that faith, passion,
and intellect must be close companions.

In Memoriam

To Nelle Morton for her continually provocative insight, honest criticism,
and nurturing friendship.

Contents

Acknowledgments

The intellectual, spiritual, and emotional contributions to this work have come from a multitude of people, only a few of whom I have space to mention. There were those who engaged me in enthusiastic conversations about the latest phase of my thinking and those who kept goading me into finishing with the question, "Is it done yet?" They all nurtured the fruition of this writing.

I am especially grateful to Thiasos, the feminist community of scholars in Claremont, California, the womb that birthed my theological voice. We spent many magical hours together thinking through our passions, learning to trust our journeys into uncharted territories, and hearing each other into liberating speech. From that group Lydia Cosentino, Susan Dunfee, Lori Krafte, and Nelle Morton were especially helpful in nourishing my new visions. Cathcrine Keller, who cofounded Thiasos, became with me a twin daughter of John Cobb and Nelle Morton. We were born into the same intellectual moment as we entered graduate school together in 1977; Catherine's sisterhood and friendship continue to be an exciting, empowering bond at the heart of my labors.

Patient support and clarity of thought to my sometimes faltering and often muddled articulations came from John Cobb and Kathleen Wicker. Much of the intelligibility of this work is due to their sympathetic listening and careful, critical suggestions. To Bernard Loomer, who did not live to see this completed book, goes much credit for recognizing the passion that lay behind my feminist anger and for pushing me into this project ten years ago, despite my misgivings.

As I have talked about this book with others, the American Asian Disciples, Asian Women Theologians Network, and Disciples Peace Fellowship provided important encouragement and communities of support and faith. Other individuals such as Rebecca Clouse, Paula Cooey, Coletta Eichenberger, Jeanine Elliott, Erik Latoni Garcia, Richard Gelwick, Claudia Highbaugh, Jay McDaniel, Carole Myscofski, Deb Pursifull, and Daryl Smith variously helped me either through feedback on early drafts, discussion about the issues, or help with later drafts. Tom Dillingham gave expert proofreading help in addition to intellectual input, and, in the final draft, Brent Schondelmeyer provided invaluable editing help which added clarity and precision to my writing.

During a recovery time from writing the major draft of the book, I took a painting course from a gifted artist, friend, colleague, and sister, Sharyn Hyatt, whose nurturing teaching helped restore my sanity and deepened my appreciation for the power of seeing in new ways. Sharyn graciously provided the a-mazing work for the front cover, *Rehem*. She painted it as we were team teaching a course called "Growing Up Female," and as she awaited, in her fourth month, a new family member, a child due nearly simultaneously with the publication of this book. I can think of no image more appropriate to depict the visual essence of my writing.

Sister Circle, the feminist spirituality group that helped me to discover and, for five years, to sustain my spiritual center, taught me that religious depth, profound connection, and liberating wholeness come from risking the breaking of old taboos, trusting myself in community with others who search for healing, and learning to venture by heart. That circle, now spun out to Europe, Australia, Asia, and North America, lives in me as a profound expectation of the power of life-giving spirit. To Yoshie, Ann, Nelle, Charlotte, Linda, Randi, Anne, Betty, Mitzi, Patty, Catherine, Linda, Joelle, Mary, and Micki—blessed be.

Introduction

We live in a brokenhearted society. Despite our scientific advances and economic affluence, suffering afflicts our world profoundly, for our new technologies permit us to threaten life as never before and our affluence has not helped the poor. Until this century, the main Christian message to the brokenhearted was the promise that, if we could bear our suffering with fortitude and faith, a new life in Jesus Christ's death and resurrection would manifest itself beyond this veil of tears. Christian piety held forth a reward. Those who believed that Jesus Christ died for their sins could participate with him in resurrection to a new life.

Faith in the resurrection must come from real glimpses of our ability to make whole our suffering world. For the work of Christian grace and love is now, and not just later. In facing squarely the suffering in our world, the social gospel, liberation, black, and feminist movements have swept in winds of change unparalleled in Christian theology since the Reformation. These movements challenge the traditional self-understanding of the church. They reject the delayed promise of heaven and seek to know the meaning of the resurrection as a lived reality rather than a faint hope. Those who suffer have proclaimed their own basis for faith, a basis that rejects passive piety. Sacrificing the present to future goals is no longer the hallmark of authentic Christian faith. This new reformation is asking whether the church can be a redemptive, transforming power in the twenty-first century if it cannot heal and liberate the brokenhearted now.[1] The work of these new movements is crucial for those who care about the fate of the church and the world.

This book looks at love and redemption from the feminist branch of the new reformation. It examines the heart of Christianity, its christology—its understanding of divine love and redemption in doctrines about Christ. For while Christ has continually been upheld as the heart of the promise of Christianity, Christ is a major problem in feminist theology. That problem has been born of an unholy trinity, father-son-holy ghost, that has cradled Christ in its patriarchal arms.

God the father has come to symbolize male dominance and the cost to women of living under sexist oppression. The father denies women their own divinely created destinies. He subordinates women to male authorities and their benevolent protection. Such paternalism sees women's status and legitimacy as determined by their relationships to men.

Many feminist theologians have dismantled this branch of the unholy trinity and proposed theologies that liberate God from patriarchy. The first two chapters of this book also examine patriarchal ideologies. They scrutinize the patriarchal roots of theology that feed our thinking and structure our relationships with each other. In doing so, I am explaining the cost to our entire society of male dominance through the loss of our capacity to see the true meaning of love. Christian theology claims that the divine incarnation in human life redeems the human condition and reveals the true nature of God (or as I prefer, God/dess) as love. That claim lies at the heart of my discussion on the power of God/dess as love. Traditional Christian theology has made self-sacrifice the highest form of love. In affirming God/dess as love, I am proposing that we see intimacy as love in its fullest form. In arguing for intimacy, I am planting a theology grounded in a feminist view of love as the basis of all power in human life.

The second branch of the unholy Trinity, the son, has been used to claim that god the father became incarnate exclusively in male form. Jesus Christ as the son is used to buttress male dominance, as Mary Daly, Rosemary Radford Ruether, and Patricia Wilson-Kastner have carefully demonstrated in their works on christology. In fact, it is Jesus' maleness, and no other of his particular human characteristics, like race, age, class, or ethnicity, that has kept women, an entire category of persons, out of full participation in the Christian community. Jesus' sex has been used to argue against the ordination of and for the subordination of women, placing Jesus out on a very shaky sexist limb. In a patriarchal culture, proclaiming salvation through the divine son implies that women must enter Christianity through male action and authority. Making masculinity normative places Christian theology directly in the path of the feminist assault on androcentrism, an ideology which defines as true of all human persons what is true of men.

Through androcentrism, the experiences and reality of women are made invisible. The son, as a model for all human behavior, no matter how prophetic, feminist, or androgynous, cannot include women. For he is still male, and no woman is allowed to represent human existence in the same inclusive way.

Doctrines of new life through the death of the son make separation and disconnection the source of reconciliation and connection. Daly has called these doctrines necrophilic because they make death the source of new life. The doctrines of salvific death do not make sense. There is no mystery here. Connection cannot come from disconnection any more than love can come from hate. Chapter 3 takes up this filial cross in the discussion of the atoning death of the son and its model of abusive relationships. I also present a feminist alternative for understanding Christ, not singly as the son, but as the full incarnation of God/dess in life-giving relationships. By expanding Christ beyond Jesus of Nazareth, we can find the true power of the redemption of human life revealed in the life-giving power of community.

The third branch of the unholy trinity seems innocuous enough. The holy ghost is the divine presence in the church. But interpretations of the biblical and doctrinal texts, supposedly inspired by the holy ghost, proclaim silence and subordination for women, the polluting nature of the female body, and the rightful exclusion of women from equality in the church. These words of the ghost haunt every attempt by women to gain full citizenship in the Christian community. This ghost has been used to protect the past at the expense of the liberation of real people in the present.

No feminist theology can afford to let the past destroy the reality of our lives today. Chapters 4 and 5 examine how we can exorcise oppressive ghosts and liberate the Gospel for our present. These chapters illuminate the liberating and healing spirit that is shrouded in unholy ghosts by examining the Gospel of Mark.

This feminist christology liberates Christ from the unholy trinity. It does so by exposing the brokenheartedness at the center of that trinity, doctrines about the life and work of Jesus Christ. These doctrines make claims about the character of being human, about what redeems us from our sinful human character, and about the power of god to resurrect us.

The heart of Christianity must be reinterpreted in nonoppressive ways if Christianity's greatest promise is not to remain its greatest problem, not just for women, but for all who seek to liberate the present. The feminist redemption of Christ must move us beyond a narrow focus on Jesus and the tyranny of the past toward forgiving, healing relationships with our world.

If Jesus is a model for self-giving, for filial obedience, for love, or for liberation, the question a Christian must ask is, "What would Jesus do or have me do in this situation?" Such a question leads the focus of feeling and action away from self-awareness, away from our inner selves, our contexts, and our history because we are not compelled to ask "How do I feel right now, how are others feeling, and what can I do to lessen all our pain and suffering in this context?" The first question focuses on reality external to us as the prime source for love and action, on obedience to ideology, conformity to heroic norms, self-sacrifice, and vicarious feelings. The second moves toward heart—toward self-possession, profound relationality, and the emergence of creative caring. The reclamation of heart is crucial to the redemption of Christ and ourselves.

Heart, as a metaphor for the human self and our capacity for intimacy, involves the union of body, spirit, reason, and passion through heart knowledge, the deepest and fullest knowing. For we know best "by heart." Heart, the center of all vital functions, is the seat of self, of energy, of loving, of compassion, of conscience, of tenderness, and of courage—the Latin *cor* means heart. To take heart is to gain courage. Our lives bloom in fullness from the heart, the core of our being, which is created and sustained by interconnection.

Heart, used unsentimentally, carries rich connotations; it suggests powerfully the various holistic dimensions of self. Heart is the center, innermost region, and most real, vital meaning and core of our lives. The human heart is symbolically the source of emotions, especially humane ones such as love, empathy, loyalty, and courage. The profoundest intellect lodges in our heart where thought is bound with integrity, insight, consciousness, and conscience. To know in our heart is to understand at heart. Memory dwells in heart, for in remembering by heart we know in ways that lie deep within us. To have a change of heart involves a shift in perspective of our whole being. In heart abides also our spirit, for faith and trust are not acts of mind, but of heart. Heart is what binds us to others, safeguards our memory, integrates all dimensions of ourselves, and empowers us to act with courage. The union of physical, emotional, and spiritual suggests itself in the very word *heart*, which also is the physical center of our bodies, their vital source. Finally, the heart encompasses the emotional and spiritual dimensions of our lives.[2]

My use of heart makes my position slightly different from feminist theologians such as Elisabeth Schüssler Fiorenza, Rosemary Radford Ruether, and Letty Russell, who emphasize the overturning of patriarchal power hierarchies. Their excellent articulation of the turning of oppressed and oppressor upside down as essential to liberation has allowed me to emphasize a different aspect of feminist work. I am seeking to turn patriarchy inside out, to reveal its ravaged, faint, fearful, broken heart, and to illuminate the power that heals heart. It is a power that allows the touching of heart to heart, a healing and touching that guide us toward a greater experience of the sacred in life.

My use of heart also distinguishes me from those feminists who have found Christianity too great a cross to bear. The decision to leave Christianity is a credible one, given its role in the reinforcement of Western patriarchy. However, when Christianity has moved into other cultural contexts, such as Asia, it has sometimes served to loosen the stranglehold of male dominance. Within those cultures, it brings a new orientation to reality, much the way that Buddhism has functioned to challenge Western culture.[3] The complexities of Christianity's functioning within different patriarchal contexts points to the intricate, shifting, evolving process of liberation in specific historical contexts. Liberation as a process undercuts the idea of liberation as an abstract goal or pure state—a kernel that can be lifted out of the messiness of concrete reality. Christianity has functioned as an iconoclastic tool of liberation and life-giving power in Latin America and the American black community. Christianity cannot simply be dismissed as hopelessly oppressive of women, unless all women are regarded as middle class and white. The liberating function of Christianity does not nullify its patriarchy, as Asian, black and Latin American feminists point out.[4] But within its patriarchy many women of color find a liberating note.

I feel, as a woman of color, that acknowledging the full extent of Christian male dominance is important to its transformation and to our being on the way toward liberation. My feminist project is to understand, in its patriarchy, how it can be reinterpreted to become nonpatriarchal. I seek both to salvage and transform Christianity.

One of my guides for transformation has been my exploration into feminist spirituality. The feminist quest for the Goddess and for wholeness outside traditional sexist worship have empowered my own spiritual journey profoundly. My explorations in feminist religious communities have nurtured spiritual parts of myself not accessible to me through the church. As much as I have found empowerment in feminist spirituality, my journeys into wholeness have brought me back repeatedly to Christianity and to the examination of my anger at the subtlety and extent of androcentrism in theological doctrines. Connections that provoke such anger are not easy to leave behind. The connections return to haunt me because Christianity has nurtured as well as wounded me.

The circumstances of my own life have compelled me, over and over, to return to my roots, to seek to understand the complex worlds that have borne me on my own journeys by heart. Combining unlikely ideas and seeing questions from odd angles result from my struggles to integrate a life lived on three continents. I am a Japanese-Puerto Rican immigrant American. I was raised in a Japanese Buddhist family until, at age six, I was brought to the United States by my Japanese mother and white, Christian stepfather, making my cultural roots Asian and American. My Asian sensibilities lie under the surface of this book like ancient stones overgrown with weeds and new grass.

Those Asian sensibilities, often in conflict with my American ones, tend to see oppositions as false polarities. In looking beyond false polarities and analytic, critical modes of thinking, I seek an intuitive, nonlinear whole. That whole involves a sensitive attunement to my own inner subjective world as the source of the compassionate healing of suffering. Both the Japanese commitment to compassion, inner insight, and generosity and the liberating power of American feminism inform my journey in this book. For I am Asian American. Oppression by both race and gender are facts of my life.

The feminist clearing of the thickets of patriarchal oppression opens ways to heal and liberate us all. The feminist struggle to transform our male-dominant society so that we might better love ourselves and each other lies at the core of my analysis of our current human condition. No assessment of the human character can ignore, without great peril, feminist analyses of male dominance. Placing those analyses at the center of my work has taught me much about brokenheartedness, which grows systemically out of paternalism, dependency, oppression, and suffering. Through feminism, I have experienced liberating love and healing wholeness.

Christian theology has tended to focus on cognitive, analytic, and often polemical methods of discourse, a noisiness that makes the quiet, inner journey to heart difficult. I believe a liberating faith lies on the borders of our thinking where heart links thinking with feeling, perception, and the body. This looking toward and from the heart is what has compelled me to turn patriarchy inside out and to examine the broken heart of male dominance. And there, in examining my own wounds, I find the power that heals and allows the touching of heart to heart, the most sacred power I know.

The complex aspects of my life come together in the identity called Asian American woman. A Japanese American woman who spent World War II in an internment camp in California tells this story about the American Asian experience: Catholics, Protestants, and Quakers in the camps worked with the imprisoned Japanese Americans to make their lives more humane. This woman was angry and bitter about her white Christian neighbors who did nothing as other Christians put her people in the camps. But these Christians in her camp made her curious, for they too were acting out of Christian conviction. In her perplexity, she decided to read the Bible. To her amazement she discovered that those who seemed to own Christianity, her oppressors, owned it illegitimately. Words about liberating captives, healing the sick, feeding the poor, and caring for orphans told her about her own life. She became a Christian because she decided the gospel did not belong to those who hurt her. Her insight is simple and profound. The past and its traditions must liberate and make whole the present. All use of the past to hurt and to oppress is illegitimate, and those who are hurt by traditions have the right to decide what makes us whole. I seek here to reveal what, in christology, can lead us toward a whole-making life.

I believe feminists of all colors will become increasingly important to the transformation of our society with our explorations into the meaning of being human. We use interdependent methods of thinking and working and bring passionate commitments to new visions of a liberated future. In our attempts to create greater intimacy, we seek to embrace the largest possible world. Feminist impulses toward inclusivity and ecumenism in the widest possible sense, while ambivalent and imperfect, are crucial for the development of depth and breadth in our visions and dreams. Those analyses, methods, and visions along with others in liberation, black, and postmodern thought, are part of our journey toward a nonpatriarchal future. It is a future yet to emerge, in which we will live and move and have our being in the wholeness of heart. This book is part of our journey together.

· 1 ·

The Character of Being Human and the Making of Human Character

To be alive today is to live with pain. For some of us, our pain is the daily struggle to survive and to find a safe place to live. Others of us work to lift oppressive barriers that silence us and batter us into submission. For those unable to hope or to find one sustaining, ennobling relationship, a quiet, desolate loneliness defines the center of our existence, a center sometimes hidden by intense, aimless activity or hollow friendships. To live with our pain without some comprehension is to exist in the denial of pain or in the overwhelming, intractable presence of it. Both lead to despair.[1]

We live in a world come of age, a world no longer innocent about the suffering human beings can inflict on each other. Auschwitz, Hiroshima, Bangladesh, Beirut, Afghanistan, and countless other places have become poignant reminders of our continuing capacity for cruelty and despair. We must understand the roots of our suffering. We require some structure of meaning that empowers us to change our world to lessen suffering. Our very survival depends upon how we come to terms with our pain, not just as individuals, but as a species. For, blinded by our self-protective fear, we have invented means to destroy our entire earth home.

Our Character as Sinfulness

The Western Christian tradition has understood the roots of our pain as sinfulness. People sin because we are sinners, that is, we have fallen from our

1

divinely created character and exist in a state of original sin. Original sin means we are self-deceptive and estranged from a right relationship to God because of unbelief and our self-centered hubris, or pride. Feminist theologians such as Valerie Saiving, Judith Plaskow, and Susan Dunfee have challenged that picture of sin by asking what sin is for those who have little pride or sense of self.

The claim that Jesus Christ and his death and resurrection are the way out of the consequences of sin has rested on particular notions of the character of being human, of the human character, and of redemption. A cornerstone in Christian descriptions of the human condition and its redemption is the claim that Jesus as the Christ represents what is of ultimate saving importance for humanity. Faith in Jesus Christ redeems us from sin and its consequences. Because we are in a state of sin, our salvation must come from our authentic encounter with and dependence upon a power outside ourselves called God. These doctrines of sin, humanity, salvation, and power are rooted in Western thought and represent the primary values of Western culture.

As a product of Western culture, our theology has been drawn largely from the philosophical traditions of Greek, Roman, German, and British thought. Feminist theorists have criticized these traditions for their androcentrism and for their emergence in and reinforcement of social-cultural systems of male dominance, systems feminists have called patriarchy. In *The Creation of Patriarchy* Gerda Lerner defines it as

> The manifestation and institutionalization of male dominance over women and children in the family and the extension of male dominance over women in society in general. It implies that men hold power in all the important institutions of society and that women are deprived of access to such power. It does *not* imply that women are either totally powerless or totally deprived of rights, influence, and resources.[2]

Christianity, according to feminist analysis, has not understood fully the human condition because it has not understood the extent to which it is involved in patriarchy. It has instead, in much of its theology, been characteristically patriarchal. Until Christianity fully faces its reinforcement of patriarchy, its analysis of the human condition will not be adequate to provide a vision of salvation for both women and men. Hence a thorough understanding of patriarchy is crucial to the development of minimally adequate theological ideas.

Patriarchy is not, I believe, a universal phenomenon, though it is virtually so. It is a social-historical product with a complex series of causes. Christianity has emerged from and been sustained in patriarchal cultures and is deeply infected with a patriarchal world view, as a number of feminists have demonstrated. In universalizing its patriarchal view of the human condition, Christian theology has blinded itself to other structures of human life. It has continued to be most blind, I believe, to abuse and pain at the heart of our society, the family, which is one of the social institutions most important to the maintenance of male dominance.

In upholding as normative the patriarchal family and its structures, Christianity has ignored the suffering of women and children at its very center and has not understood the implications of patriarchy for those who live within such structures. In the United States suicide is the second most common form of death among teenagers; one in every five children grows up in poverty; one in every three women will be raped as an adult, one in every four daughters and one in every eight sons are molested by the age of eighteen; and every thirty-nine seconds a woman is battered in her own home. Homicide is the fifth leading cause of death for American children ages one through eighteen and 1.4 million children annually, ages three through seventeen, are physically abused. Adrienne Rich has called the family home the most dangerous place in America for women. Violence is more common than love and respect.[3] In ignoring the suffering caused by the patriarchal family, Christian theology has painted a nostalgic and untrue picture of that family and based much of its theology on its nostalgia.[4] While patriarchy is not the only cause of human evil and suffering, in the social-historical religion called Christianity, it is a central factor. I believe we must understand the depth to which the patriarchal family is involved in our theological assumptions if we are to understand suffering fully.

My placing of the family at the core of this feminist work on christology, rather than race, gender, and class, reflects my assumption that the major key to the continuation of patriarchy and to our ability to transform our patriarchal society lies with the family. I also believe that our consciousness and knowledge of race, gender, and class, for good or ill, are born within and taught first in family structures. In addition, the many various forms of the patriarchal family, during the several millennia that patriarchy has existed, have been the cornerstone of male dominance, as well as the primary sphere of activity for women. Family here means the persons with whom we develop the interpersonal bonds that shape us from birth until death, bonds formed with the primary persons from whom we learn what it means to be ourselves, to belong to a group, and to relate to others and to a larger world. If we are to understand fully what it means to be human, we must see what the oppression of women costs our families and society, as well as what the agency of women teaches us about nurturing life and about the nature of close human relationships.

My focus on the family is inextricable from my conviction that we are fundamentally relationship-seeking beings. We internalize most deeply and powerfully our earliest relationships, from which come our ability or inability to internalize later loves and losses, to coexist humanely with others, and to continue to flourish and grow as persons. Hence healthy, loving, and supportive families are crucial to nurture compassionate, ethical persons and create sane and just societies. Family is the fundamentally necessary factor for the building of human character and for the development of all societies, including ours.

Finally, images of the patriarchal family are omnipresent in theology and especially christology. The patriarchal family is one in which a dominant male is primarily responsible for providing for all those under his authority who are dependent upon him. From trinitarian images of father-son-spirit to doctrines of the death of the only begotten son, patriarchal family relationships are the bricks of the patriarch's theological house of worship. Those bricks include punitive ingredients such as the divine judgment on disobedient, wayward children; nostalgic, sentimental ingredients such as the loving, forgiving father; and hierarchical marriage ingredients such as the bridegroom Christ and the bride church. The unquestioned truth and validity of patriarchal family structures litter the entire corpus of Christian theology, as well as the biblical text. This assumption of validity is fundamentally challenged by the feminist analysis of patriarchy.

The quality of care given to children is crucial to whether they grow into loving persons or destructive adults capable of monstrous acts. That care takes place in the family, which is itself shaped by its society. The fragility of their earliest existence makes children easily broken. In a patriarchal society, children must be nurtured into wholeness with little social support for such nurturing.

A number of global studies of gender stratification highlight a complex series of factors that lead to the emergence of male dominance and societies that create more hostile and insecure selves. The factors producing and supporting male dominance are multiple and interrelated, but central is the control of women's reproductive powers and, with that, the family, the cornerstone of patriarchy. Religious ideas evolve to reflect patriarchal social structures. Male dominance is supported by masculine deities, a male clerical class, and ideologies of female subordination, including women's physical weakness and uncleanness, and emotional and moral inferiority.[5]

With the development of such gender and class stratified societies, separate roles, functions, and orientations to reality emerge for women and men. Differences between women and men have been both inflicted by and noticed in Western culture. However, the male academic response to such differences, beginning with Hesiod and Aristotle, has been to assume that men characterize humanness and that women are deficient in that respect. With this androcentric bias, women are consistently subordinated to men in every academic discipline. The keystone of any feminist theory is the rejection of this subordination.

Because every issue in our society affects women, a narrow disciplinary study of any problem affecting women is virtually impossible. Feminist theory demonstrates this breadth by its inherently interdisciplinary nature. While the main objective in this chapter is to develop a feminist theological understanding of the character of being human that will lay a foundation for subsequent chapters, the sources I use include a variety of disciplines such as sociology, anthropology, psychology, literature, and theology. The interplay of these disciplines is helpful in understanding human existence because they supplement a largely androcentric theological tradition.[6]

An accurate understanding of patriarchy as it continues to exist in modern form is an important background to the shaping of feminist theology. Lerner and other feminist theorists such as Zillah Eisenstein and Peggy Reeves Sanday insist on the importance of studying the history and development of patriarchy so that we can obtain an accurate analysis of women's situations and formulate empowering theories. In studying our prepatriarchal and patriarchal past, Lerner seeks to find how women have been, and continue to be, agents in the building of civilization, not simply its victims, and to discover how we can be a shaping force in the creation of a nonpatriarchal future. While I believe this prehistoric and historic exploration is important, other feminists have done it well. The focus of this study will be the factors that continue to characterize male dominance today. In setting forth a feminist analysis of the character of human existence, I am exploring the roots of suffering in American society, especially as patriarchy is a factor in such suffering, but such an analysis will have, I hope, points of applicability in other patriarchal cultures.

The Shallowness of Sinfulness

Sinfulness, as a category within Christian analyses of humanity, is tied to the reinforcement of patriarchal theology. That reinforcement is hooked to the structure of the patriarchal family with mothers at its center. Sinfulness is aligned with blame, punishment, and guilt, and blame has usually been assigned to woman as the originator of sin, or to our maternal, organic birth which must be transcended by a higher, spiritual birth. While such assignation of blame may absolve individual believers of guilt, it carries undertones of both misogyny and self-hate for it puts persons in inner conflict with themselves.

In *Beyond God the Father* Mary Daly discusses at length the projection of evil on to woman, and Rosemary Ruether and Patricia Wilson-Kastner address the use of woman to explain evil. Ruether further discusses dualistic self-hate that is implicit in the division between the good self and evil self, a division that requires the dismemberment of the self, rather than a profound self-acceptance. In discussing the uniting of misogyny and self-hate in the traditional notions of evil, Ruether states in *Sexism and God-Talk*:

> If sexism is both violence and violation to women's bodily integrity, humanity, and capacity for full selfhood, sexism is also the distortion of male humanity. Although males have sought to monopolize the most valued human tasks, to keep for themselves both the highest culture and the leisure that allows the pursuit of culture and creativity, they have not thereby succeeded in actualizing a humanity that we should generally want to emulate. Both in its brutality and in its intellectual abstractionism, sexism distorts male humanity and thereby distorts the whole human enterprise. If the distortion of female humanity is a tragedy of victimization at many points, the distortion of male humanity is an endemic disease that both humanity and the planet itself may not long survive without dramatic conversion.[7]

The rejection of feared aspects of the self, labeled as evil or feminine, results in the absence of self-awareness and self-acceptance.

Modern discussions of sinfulness tend to describe it as alienation which emerges through self-assertion and the denial of the self's dependence on God. Sinfulness is understood to be a state that is prior to the particular relationships that shape human beings. In the face of political oppressions, vast economic inequities, wars, and the current threat of global suicide by nuclear destruction, Christian theologians have stepped back from their nineteenth-century optimism about human nature to a stronger emphasis on the pervasiveness of human sin and on the need for us to acknowledge our sinful state and responsibility for evil. Our sophisticated, intricate society and its technology have enabled us to create increasingly original forms of sin.

Western theology has followed Augustine in identifying the human condition as original sin. Until the last decade feminist studies of patriarchy have not influenced discussions of the human condition. These studies should inform our understanding of the human condition because they provide a new, important perspective useful to theological reflection. While feminists are not naive about human evil and suffering, we understand sin as historically and socially produced, which requires us to take responsibility for understanding and stopping oppression and suffering.

I believe understanding sin as damage enhances responsibility and healing instead of miring us in blame and guilt. I am suggesting that sinfulness is neither a state that comes inevitably with birth nor something that permeates all human existence, but a symptom of the unavoidably relational nature of human existence through which we come to be damaged and damage others. Our attempts to avoid that radically relational nature—a thoroughly contingent existence which embeds us in history and society—emerge from our inability to face our own pain and be healed. If we begin with an understanding that we are intimately connected, constituted by our relationships ontologically, that is, as a basic unavoidable principle of existence, we can understand our brokenness as a consequence of our relational existence. This ontological relational existence, the heart of our being, is our life source, our original grace. But we are, by nature, vulnerable, easily damaged, and that vulnerability is both the sign of our connectedness and the source of the damage that leads us to sin.

Sin emerges because our relationships have the capacity to destroy us and we participate in destruction when we seek to destroy ourselves or others. Hence sin is a sign of our brokenheartedness, of how damaged we are, not of how evil, willfully disobedient, and culpable we are. Sin is not something to be punished, but something to be healed. That we exist at all is a sign that the destructive relationships of our lives have not been final and that we have the responsibility of acknowledging our connectedness to others and our commitment to the creation of right relationships.

While modern discussions of sin are not intended to impart blame or evoke guilt, but are supposed to free us to be self-accepting without the necessity for being good or perfect, feminist discussions of sin assert that our doctrines of sin do not lead to enhanced self-acceptance for women.[8] In addition, the admission of our powerlessness in the face of the magnitude of human evil finally leaves us impotent to take responsibility for our own evil except through dependence on a "higher" power. The acknowledgement of our sinful nature and dependence on divine power have not stopped the church and Christian nations from creating some of the most oppressive societies in history, as theologians are quick to acknowledge. We have found little to pull us out of the increasing velocity of the vortex sucking us into global death.

I take human evil and suffering and their consequences seriously, but I do not believe most doctrines of sin go deep enough to the roots of our ability to hurt ourselves and each other. For all their discussions of pride, evil, alienation, greed, racism, war, and so on, Christians have not been able to deal fully with the presence of evil in our own patriarchal hearts. Hence churches have tended not to initiate actions to understand or stop the evils that lie closest to the heart of society, the family—evils such as child abuse, battering, rape, incest, or forced pregnancy and sterilization. It has taken feminists to call attention, repeatedly, to these issues. Even when Christians have addressed such problems as poverty and oppression, our approach is often benignly paternalistic. It is far safer to identify with victims and want to help them than to look at our own participation in systems of oppression and our responsibility for changing ourselves and the systems from which we benefit. The Christian attitude toward charity is often built on the idea of the superior helping the inferior, which locks paternalism into the relationship. Rather than seeing our capacity to give to the poor as part of a social-economic system that produces poverty and hunger, much Christian charity is designed to help others into the exploitive system. Until liberation, black, and feminist theologians began to speak of the self-empowerment of the oppressed, the oppressed were largely seen as victims to be acted upon rather than as a presence in the church that radically challenged its self-identity.[9]

Through the profound acknowledgement of our primal interrelatedness we can begin to find grace and to embrace and to heal the damage and suffering of our deepest selves and our society. Original grace is this healing gift, a reality that begins at birth. I search for theological images and ideas that will help us embrace the fullest possible life through the ultimate claim relationships make on our very being. I will explore, in the context of original grace, the damage to self, to heart, that is a consequence of patriarchy, damage that can be understood theologically as one major violation of original grace. I believe it is our damage—in which one major factor is patriarchy—that has produced a doctrine of sin as a description of our original human state. The existence of that category requires us to misplace divine incarnation and human redemption in someone else's perfection and heroic action, or in a power outside ourselves that helps us transcend the concrete realities of our lives. Believing in our own goodness does not eliminate our need to take responsibility for our own capacities for evil. In fact, I believe that self-acceptance and attention to all our feelings and impulses empower us to change, to heal ourselves, and to understand the roots of evil.

The Depths of Our Damage

Feminist psychologists have begun to research the domestic arena of child-rearing for clues to the maintenance of patriarchy. Childhood has been largely neglected in androcentric studies of human life until the rise of psychoanalysis. Especially important to American feminist psychology has been the development of object-relations theory. While accepting the basic psychoanalytic insight that infancy and early childhood are essential periods for personality formation, object-relations theorists supplant the traditional Freudian drive-conflict and ego-centered model of human development with one of needs-deprivation. Their holistic, integrated idea of the human self is based in wider shaping influences on the self. These influences that shape personality include the family, society, and culture. Object-relations theory asserts that the self is formed by the internalization of its relationships. As internalized objects, relationships become the basic ingredients from which a sense of self is shaped. Hence the self is relationship-seeking activity. Feminist object-relations theorists have been occupied with understanding childhood, gender difference in patriarchal society, and the development of women's sense of self, given our current society. [10]

Alice Miller focuses her object-relations analysis on the narcissistic stage of life, the earliest beginnings of infant care and development. [11] Miller's work on early self-development helps us understand better the role of gender in the later stages of the formation of selves under patriarchy. According to Miller, the self is a set of capacities born into each individual uniquely at birth. These capacities involve the ability to feel one's own physical, emotional, and sensory needs, to make those needs known, and to receive through the body, senses, and feelings, the world outside the self. How a self's feelings, thoughts, perceptions, and physical awareness are developed and shaped depends on the world into which the self is born and how that world is able to facilitate the self's development. Just as the physical body never remains the same, the perceptions, feelings, and thoughts of the self also mature and develop through the expression, acknowledgement, and integration of all of the self's capacities. The development of a healthy self requires care, protection, security, touching, tenderness, and being respected as a separate self.

The integrative, holistic, and complex definition of experience as the basis of self in object-relations theory parallels, to some extent, Alfred North Whitehead's philosophical use of the word *feeling* in *Process and Reality*. For Whitehead, feeling involves the way we include through all forms of perception and reception—conscious and unconscious, cognitive and emotional, spiritual and physical—all our past experiences. Since he is laying a metaphysical groundwork for all experience, Whitehead does not discuss the impact of hierarchical and controlling power on the development of feeling. This political and psychological analysis is full-blown in Miller who asserts that our past world can impinge severely on the full and healthy development of human feeling in its broadest, most inclusive sense.

Miller finds little evidence that the complex needs of the self have been, or can be, met adequately in Euro-American culture. Instead, the dependency of children is exploited by adults for their own needs, producing damage that has lifelong effects because children produce false selves that mirror adult needs and neuroses. In addition, because adults tend to see children as extensions of their own needs, society usually exonerates adults and blames children for their own abuse.

The infant's "true" self is the tactile, sensory, feeling self that makes its needs known and receives into itself the world around it. Infancy and early childhood are, according to object-relations theory, crucial periods for the enhanced development of the true self or its damage and the creation of a false one. My use of "heart" parallels Miller's "true self." The range and depth of experience included in the term self is the activity and energy of heart such that the false self is the activity of a broken heart. As long as an infant is nurtured by others who can satisfy its sensory needs and who can acknowledge, positively confirm, and receive its feelings, no matter what the feelings, the infant will not lose touch with its true self. However, if the primary nurturer, most often a mother, has been taught to fear certain feelings as bad, especially feelings such as sexuality, sensuality, anger, and jealousy, the infant senses the unconscious clues of repression and fear and loses touch with the same feelings.

In referring to primary nurturers, and especially mothers, Miller repeatedly cautions against the tendency, even in psychoanalysis, when it is not feminist psychoanalysis, to affix blame to mothers. While realizing our own pain may involve, at some point, a healthy rage at our parents, Miller asserts that self-awareness comes with grief and the realization that those who are themselves wounded wound others. Such a realization allows us compassion for others as we take responsibility for our own woundedness. Hence Miller's work on child abuse and the creation of false selves is not intended as child-rearing advice. She explicitly disavows the adviser role. Instead she is seeking to heal the wounded child in us, and I believe her message reaches us most deeply when we listen to her, not as adults, but as those hurt children buried inside us.

Burying powerful passions in infancy means a tragic loss of connection to any intense feeling. The infant must deny its feeling self. The true self is buried by parental control, no matter how benign, because the infant self is fused with the mother or primary nurturer. With such fusion the two relate to each other as extensions of themselves.

Parents who have been denied their true selves and have not reclaimed them as adults have not had their own deepest needs for love and acceptance met. Miller states that parents, who act out of their own false selves, will see their children as beings who can be shaped to love them as they want to be loved or as beings who can be molded into the person they have always wanted to be. Doing so protects parents from their own sense of loneliness and failure. These parents will often treat their children in what they believe are loving ways, "stoning [them] with kisses," as Miller says, or using positive reinforcement. However, the primary orientation is toward use and control. Parents who perceive children as beings to be shaped and controlled experience their children as extensions of themselves, rather than as separate beings. This orientation is so common in our culture, it is seen as a norm.

Children, to gain the approval and love of their parents, respond by giving them what they want. Children have little choice; for love is as essential as food. Children learn to bury their own needs and feelings when no one is available to receive them and to hear their experiences into objective existence. Such children as adults will be highly empathetic and sensitive to the needs and feelings of others but unable to admit or feel their own. Or they will be achievement oriented, if achievement wins approval. The feelings of relief and respect gained by success through achievement replace the buried feelings of the true self. In addition to the focus on approval and success, false selves must deny childhood ambivalence and create a nostalgic, idealized view of their parents and childhood. False selves require a nostalgic past to keep feelings hidden. As long as adults with false selves, oriented toward others, can guarantee the approval of others through empathy or achievement, they may avoid being haunted by the pain that produces a false self. However, depression constantly lurks behind loss or failure as the clearest clue that the true feeling self is lost.

Miller's terms "true" and "false" self sound somewhat dualistic, as if they were opposites. However, in her theory the false self is a dynamic of and clue to the true self and its defenses against the deprivation of its needs. The false self protects the damaged true self and masks it. My use of heart and broken heart also implies the intimacy of our woundedness and how it manifests itself. A false self helps us avoid facing the brokenheartedness that afflicts us at such an early and vulnerable stage of our lives.

If parents control children in more punitive or violent ways, the consequences are far more devastating in the creation of false selves and to the possibility of reclaiming the true self. Miller contends that all punishment damages children's selves by shutting down their capacity to feel. The humiliation of children through abuse has been regarded as the means to shape children "for their own good." But such methods produce intense pain and suffering. Without someone to confirm their feelings of suffering from the humiliation of punishment, children must bury their pain; for children cannot integrate experiences alone. Isolation is too terrifying and love too consuming a need. As adults, damaged children will split off their own pain and project it upon others by punishing their own children or victimizing others weaker than themselves, a pattern that parallels masculine identity in patriarchal societies that raise men to be dominant and aggressive and that produce powerful cultural patterns of racism, sexism, homophobia, and xenophobia. As long as the pain and humiliation remain buried, the person will be unable to empathize with another's pain or identify with victims of oppression.

Miller's analysis does not specifically cover gender. In examining gender we can see feminine tendencies toward seeking relationships of dependency that repeat the abusive punishments of childhood. The pain of the broken heart is hidden from conscious awareness and, so, is reenacted. Whether the reenactment of abuse is inflicted upon others or the self, the adult will blame the abuse on the abused. Without someone to notice the truth under the reenactment, the abuse is repeated.

Most early punishment is tied to bodily deprivation or pain. Children deny the feelings they receive through their bodies, especially feelings that are associated with their earliest suffering. The adult false self tries to ignore the body, pretends it is higher than and separate from its own embodied existence. Aspects of femaleness that most compel attention to an embodiedness that is linked to vulnerability and feeling, menstruation and birthing, for example, are regarded in male-dominant societies as unclean and defiling. Rejection of the body's vulnerability is also a necessary attribute for warriors in patriarchal societies, a skill taught to those in basic training in the military. Hence things that lead away from or conquer the body—a strong will, spirituality, and intellect, for example—are prized as higher ways to truth.

In the most extreme denials of the body, the false self will use physically destructive means to damage or destroy the body because the body cries out to be acknowledged as an aspect of the true self. As Miller states in *Thou Shalt Not Be Aware*:

> The truth about our childhood is stored up in our body, and although we can repress it, we can never alter it. Our intellect can be deceived, our feelings manipulated, our perceptions confused, and our body tricked with medication. But someday the body will present its bill, for it will accept no compromises or excuses, and it will not stop tormenting us until we stop evading the truth. [p. 318]

The false self, the one with the broken heart, manifests itself in many ways. It rests its self-esteem in winning approval from significant others by empathetic union and/or by success and achievement. In either case, the false self is maintained by its dependence on others. Also, the brokenhearted self has lost the capacity to feel intense passions, and so is haunted by depression. This self denies sensuality and tries to transcend the body. It will, in addition, often idealize its parents and past, and place blame for abuse on victims. Finally, it will seek to reproduce itself in others over whom it has control.

Well-meaning parents use control techniques to train their children, techniques including deprivation of physical or emotional needs, entrapment, manipulation, isolation, humiliation, embarrassment, cruelty, and physical pain. These techniques are supposed to teach children love, respect for others, honesty, self-respect, kindness, a love of truth, and the values of freedom and nonviolence. With such contradictory messages, *the only clear lesson is the value of power and authority*. Children learn that status and the degree of dominance we possess determine whether our actions are judged good or bad. Hence, the more parents control and punish children, the more children will "behave" only when they fear a higher, punitive authority, and the more adults so raised will seek dominance as self-protection and as an opportunity to control others. In addition, they will seek to protect authority from criticism and to educate all those under their control to respect authority. This system is power understood as dominance.

The Character of Male and Female

If we compare the creation of false selves with feminist analyses of the development of masculine and feminine social identity, we can begin, I think, to see that gender-linked views of self are largely culturally created and linked to the dynamics of false selves. Understanding the origins of patriarchy and gender difference is important for exposing stereotyped gender-linked selves in our society as the product of male dominance. While Miller does not focus her work on gender difference, her claims about control, combined with Nancy Chodorow's thesis in *The Reproduction of Mothering* about the creation of femininity and masculinity, imply that one of the main factors in creating gender differences in our culture is control-oriented parenting, the kind of parenting characteristic of patriarchal society.

In *The Reproduction of Mothering* Chodorow explains modern forms of gender difference found in the Western white nuclear family by examining the preoedipal and oedipal stages of human development that follow the narcissistic stage and seem to be the stages when gender issues emerge. She describes the Western adult masculine self as sharply ego-identified and as oriented toward goals, tasks, and rules. In the larger social picture of male-dominant societies, men must be socialized for achievement and for nondomestic tasks. Chodorow believes males develop feelings of masculinity largely over and against femininity that is seen as negative. Through a strong emphasis on individuation they acquire more defensive, rigid ego boundaries. She sees masculine identity as based on differentiation and separation from others, on generalized, abstract categories that define masculine roles, on the rejection of femininity, and on the denial of physical and emotional vulnerability and affective relation. The masculine self sees himself as needing to remain apart from relationships and affiliation, as proving his success in competitive contexts, and as becoming mature through the achievement of autonomy.

The feminine self is characterized by Chodorow as highly focused on affiliation and affective relationships. Females develop a sense of identity by connection to and dependence on others and pay closer attention to their day-to-day environment. Feminine identity feels itself incomplete without a complex of relationships of differing kinds. The feminine self avoids open conflict and competition and feels herself confirmed in the capacity to nurture others—to be attuned to and to seek to meet the needs of others.

These divergent views of self emerge because the primary caretakers of all infants and young children are most often females. Chodorow contends these early relationships in nuclear families are necessarily intense because of their narrowness. Hence males are forced to develop gender identity by separation and females by bonding. She concludes that the sex-role stereotyping in the family structures of our culture reproduces the two views of self. In addition, Chodorow asserts that extremely divergent, exaggerated, and neurotic forms of masculine and feminine identity occur when the primary caretaker is control oriented. The more controlling and emotionally needy the mother, the more exaggerated the masculine or feminine identity. This system of gender production contains its own implosive self-destruction, according to Chodorow, because the system produces unhappy, unstable selves who have different orientations to intimacy and emotional needs and exploit those over whom they have control.

In discussing narcissism, Miller does not refer to gender problems. Chodorow acknowledges their emergence first in the preoedipal stage. Adults impose them early or retroactively apply them, but neither Miller nor Chodorow believes they are part of the earliest structures of the self. If the narcissistic stage precedes gender identity formation, the gender of the primary nurturer may only become crucial as the child becomes aware of the importance of gender distinctions in a culture preoccupied with gender difference. Until then, the crucial factors for the health of the self are emotionally healthy nurturers and the absence of control and punishment. The extent of early damage to the self manifests itself later, in our patriarchal culture, through stereotyped gender roles that maintain the dualistic, hierarchical, and exploitive male-dominant power systems in our society.

The Christian notion of original sin, based in traditional, dualistic assumptions about good and evil and patriarchal notions of obedience and disobedience, claims that we are born with a tragic flaw that we do not choose, but for which we bear the penalty if we do not take responsibility for the flaw that results in evil. At the same time we are powerless alone to remove the penalty for our flaw and, therefore, must rely on a higher power whose pure goodness and grace pardon us from the penalty.

Theological dualisms undergird structures of dominance. Dualisms are reactions to abuse that produce the need for a more rigid, controllable universe. The dualisms split matter from spirit, darkness from light, good from evil, body from soul, feeling from reason, and male from female. Such dualisms are part of the religious ideologies that support male-dominant societies. The maintenance of such ideologies does not lead to the transformation of patriarchy, and a dualistic dichotomizing of reality is not necessary to spirituality or more true of ultimate reality. Instead such dualisms point to damaged selves.

Original Grace and the Making of Human Character

Because the very existence of heart is basic to the structure of human life itself and is the basis of our being broken in relationships, we require connections if we are to acknowledge our own broken heart and be healed. At the earliest part of our lives we are dependent on the loving power of others to nurture us. Their failure to do so has serious consequences. We are broken by the world of our relationships before we are able to defend ourselves. It is not a damage we willfully choose. Those who damage us do not have the power to heal us, for they themselves are not healed. To be healed, we must take the responsibility for recognizing our own damage by following our hearts to the relationships that will empower our self-healing. In living by heart, we are called not to absolve ourselves of the consequences of an inherited flaw. We are called to remember our own brokenheartedness, the extent of our vulnerability, and the depth of our need for relationships. Hence we are called not to dependence on a power outside ourselves, but to an exploration of the depths of our most inner, personal selves as the root of our connections to all others.

Miller's reliance on psychoanalysis makes her discussion of self sound essentialist. However, her concept when placed in a nonessentialist, relational ontology makes clearer sense. The self is a technical term in Miller, but she uses it holistically as a concept which integrates the complex elements of a person. The self is an achievement of our relationality, structured in our existence from birth, as our ever-changing physical existence is a structured reality at birth. That ontological structure need not be seen as an essence of self that endures through space and time, but as the fundamental character of the self recreated in every given moment by both its relationships and a sustained recollection of its past. Hence the self only exists in relationships as it focuses and structures those relationships. The self, the heart, therefore is recreated continuously through feeling, connectedness, and memory.

Heart is our original grace. In exploring the depths of heart we find incarnate in ourselves the divine reality of connection, of love. The grace we find through heart reveals the incarnate graciousness, generosity, and love necessary to human life. *But the heart's strength lies in its fragility.* To be born so open to the presence of others in the world gives us the enormous, creative capacity to make life whole. Yet such openness means that the terrifying and destructive factors of life are also taken into the self, a self that then requires loving presence to be restored to grace. Finding our heart requires a loving presence who helps the search, who is not afraid of the painfulness of the search, and who can mirror back our buried and broken heart, returning us to a healing memory of our earliest pain and need for love. This loving presence and healing memory carry the profoundest meanings of forgiveness and remembrance.

Finding our heart means remembering how we have been damaged. It means facing the past squarely, ambivalent and whole, without nostalgia, without romantic heroes and heroines, and without numbness. Nostalgia, romance, and numbness block memory and anger, both crucial avenues into heart. Memory and anger open us to our fullest self-acceptance and deepest passions. The pain and poignancy of such honest facing of the past is vividly expressed in Judy Grahn's poem *Descent to the Roses of the Family*, subtitled *Open Letter to My Brother on the Subject of Family Pride*, in which she states,

> When we see a child helpless before us
> we are likely to blossom into rage,
> a stick planted into the dirt of experience.
> We turn fury, judge and jury,
> our arms fall and rise.
> Whips shape our tongues.
> All we have known
> we pass on.
>
> This is the legacy of the white race
> that I will remember long after my death:

that it beats its children
that it blunts itself with alcohol
that its women suffer from a blight: passivity
that it carries a gun.

. . . .

This is the legacy of the white rose
that I will remember long after my death:
that its beaten children beat their children
that it calls alcohol "spirits"
that its women offer their passivity to their families
like a whip.

. . . .

no one has ever robbed me

. . . .

as this has robbed me

. . . .

my absence to myself, my deafness,
my absence to love
lifted only by some meanness, some anger

. . . .

rousing me at last
. . . to some feeling,
enough to continue.

. . . . . .

you tell me to get a gun—

. . . .

. . . I am angry.

. . . . .

Who can I shoot that can return my childhood to me?

. . . .

I'm most afraid of living with torment all my life.
I'm completely afraid of my own passivity.
Who, besides myself, can I shoot to solve any of this?

[from sections 1, 5, and 7]

Grahn describes how the evocation of such feeling and memory stopped her writing for months. It is one of the most courageous poems I have read. Throughout the poem Grahn integrates images of self-hate and violence into an honest quest for healing and self-acceptance through her search to stop the passing on of her family's atrocities. She seeks to do so by taking responsibility for her anger and through her desire to connect to her brother who feels lost to her in his violent white pride. Grahn's poem suggests the link between pride, anger, and nostalgia. In identifying sin as pride, Christian theology rightly undercuts the angry violence suppressed behind a false nostalgic picture of the self. However, in reaching for the underside, theology confuses the self-abnegation and humiliation that produce pride with the healing and self-affirmation, the grace, that come from legitimate anger and honest memory. For all anger has been condemned as sin, especially for women.

Anger that we integrate, rather than vent on others, leads us to self-assertion and self-acceptance. It allows us to perceive ourselves as distinct, to claim our own feelings, to heal our pain, and to find our own centered existence. Hence anger is a way to intimacy and loving, if it is understood to contain clues to our own pain. In acknowledging anger, we are able to move through anger to self-acceptance and compassion. Then we are capable of the fullest possible relationships, because we bring a self-aware, centered self to any relationship. We bring heart.

Anger is a key to both love and nonviolence, and it is pivotal to self-affirmation and liberation.[12] It is the healthy response of a self to violation and a crucial avenue to self-acceptance and acceptance of others. But this anger must be deeply personal, tied intimately to its roots in experience. This anger, when we take responsibility for it as part of our own damage, leads to mourning the loss of self and to the first steps to reclaiming self and intimacy.

In "On Anger" Barbara Deming, a feminist pacifist, describes this anger, based in hurt and grief, as often unsure of itself; and out of its instability and the extent of its pain, it can be explosive in its destructiveness. It is extremely powerful because it rests in the most important energy of all: the need for self-affirmation and for connection. It rises from the center of our being, raw, shaking, and hopeful. We are frightened by it because it means the loss of control and the experience of our own pain. It emerges from the pain and is often mixed with fear, which blocks our ability to feel pain. If this anger cannot emerge, we cannot love ourselves or connect fully with others. But this anger must reveal our own personal abuse or it will not be an empowering clue to ourselves, and it must emerge in connectedness. Deming cautions against what she calls "anger by analogy" and a too private view of pain:

One way . . . we avoid looking at the anger that most afflicts us, one way we find of affirming our pride *without* facing its anger (which we sense can overwhelm us) is by resisting the oppression of that pride as it were by analogy. . . . I am sure this is true for many of you who are white who joined the struggle against racism. I am not suggesting that we abandon any of the struggles that we have been taking part in. I am suggesting that if we take upon ourselves the further struggle of confronting our own most particular, own personal oppression, we will find ourselves better able to wage those struggles too—because of a more conscious solidarity. Confronting oppression, I mean, in the company of others—for what seems deeply personal is in truth deeply political. [p. 216]

Harriett Lerner in *The Dance of Anger* believes anger is the crucial first step in developing self-awareness. Lerner's discussion of gender difference claims that venting anger is acceptable masculine behavior and unacceptable feminine behavior. A son's anger puts him in a reactive separated position from a too fused, or too emotionally attached, mother. For a daughter, a too-fused mother produces a lack of self-differentiation because they are both females. A daughter fused to her mother will feel hurt or guilt as replacements for anger because hurt and guilt restore dependence. In masculine separation or feminine dependency, once again, we see that it is the fusion of selves, rather than the self-acceptance and respect for others of differentiated selves, that produces both the extremes of angry, rebellious males and passive, compliant females. Anger for many women is a crucial step in differentiating themselves from relationships that are too fused for distinct selves to exist. But the explosiveness of anger makes it easy to vent, which is not enough. Grahn's poetic images of violence and a gun and her refusal to shoot others with her anger expose the ultimate futility of venting anger.

The difficulty, for many women, of even acknowledging anger lies with strong social taboos against being angry. Women are supposed to be nurturing, nice, kind, and compliant. In *Sexism and God-Talk* Ruether discusses the impact on conservative Christian women of the identification of sin with anger and pride and virtue with humility and self-abnegation, an identification which reinforces female subjugation. Audre Lorde in an essay on anger in *Sister Outsider* discusses her experience of other women's projection of anger onto her as a black woman.

After I read from my work entitled "Poems for Women in Rage," a white woman asks me: "Are you going to do anything with how we can deal directly with *our* anger? I feel it's so important." I ask, "How do you use *your* rage?" And then I have to turn away from the blank look in her eyes, before she can invite me to participate in her own annihilation. I do not exist to feel her anger for her. [p. 125]

Anger that frees us to claim ourselves must be recognized and embraced as an aspect of ourselves. In embracing it, rather than in allowing others to feel our anger for us or in venting it on others, anger can become an important tool that helps us understand our own pain and to determine what, in our relationships, is acceptable or unacceptable for our well-being. The point of the recognition of such anger is not primarily to judge or change others, though in a relational world a change in ourselves will inevitably affect others, but to understand ourselves and to change from a reliance on a false, too-fused self to a grounding in the true self and in what hurts that self.

In *The Fact of a Door Frame* Adrienne Rich describes the union of anger and tenderness, twin angels that breathe in her: "Anger and tenderness: the spider's genius/to spin and weave in the same action/from her own body, anywhere—/even from a broken web" (p.274). In her vision of healing through life-giving feeling, Rich connects anger and tenderness with the body. In *Of Woman Born* Rich describes what it means to reclaim a relationship to our bodies as an aspect of ourselves.

Fear and hatred of our bodies has often crippled our brains. . . . We need to imagine a world in which . . . women will truly create new life, bringing forth . . . the visions, and the thinking necessary to sustain, console, and alter human existence—a new relationship to the universe. Sexuality, politics, intelligence, power, motherhood, work, community, intimacy will develop new meanings; thinking itself will be transformed. This is where we have to begin. [pp. 291–92]

Buried anger is closely tied to the body because the body is the home of the heart. Bodies are our first, closest, and most powerful connection to both ourselves and all else. The loving touch of flesh upon flesh is the first reassurance that one is a self in a world of caring selves. Through our experiences of pain and humiliation, we learn to control and ignore the body; and any embodied contact with the world becomes ambivalent. The false self learns to fear sensuality and hate the body, turning anger inward. Reclamation of the body is part of the reclamation of self as awareness of physical pain and stress can become important clues to psychic and spiritual distress.

The reclamation of the body has been a major theme of feminism from its participation in the popular health movement in the early nineteenth century and its temperance struggle against alcohol abuse to the current feminist women's health movement, antirape and antibattering activism, poverty research, and fight for reproductive rights. The defiance of male dominance in feminism means a woman's right to determine the destiny of her own body and its health and the healing of the whole person. The feminist emphasis on connectedness, wholeness, and affirmation of women's bodies and life cycle are closely tied to spiritual depth, relationship, and power. Recent feminist interest in spirituality has focused on the union of resistance to patriarchy and the need for wholeness. Some women have reclaimed ancient goddesses as metaphors of a holistic, organic orientation to life that included the affirmation of women's bodily functions, sensuality, connectedness, life-giving powers, and knowledge of healing. Feminist spirituality is both radically political and deeply personal, uniting the struggle of women to free themselves from male dominance and the need for personal, bodily integrity. Healing and liberation are the activities of that struggle.

Neither healing nor liberation of the whole self—body, mind, spirit, and feelings—is possible without memory, a memory that is comprehensive, honest, and discerning. Feminist research on child abuse and incest reveals the extent to which early physical and emotional pain can be forgotten and yet have lasting consequences on adult behavior and self-esteem. Feminist research indicates that women who have been raped as children repress memories of molestation but continue as adults to have very low self-esteem and highly ambivalent relationships with men. Childhood sexual abuse can produce substance abuse, depression, prostitution, self-labeling as bitch or whore, and the attribution of greater danger to male sexuality. I have personally observed instances, with students, some of them male, and with adult women of various ages in supportive contexts, of breaking through the amnesia of their past experiences of molestation in childhood. Their remembering, their *anamnesis*, was frightening, painful, illuminating, and, ultimately, an important opening into healing and empowerment as each struggled to understand this awesome memory of pain. Being part of a community of support that opened space for the memory to surface, that accepted their complex feelings, and that empathized with their struggle to understand what had happened were important aspects of beginning the healing process. Without a safe and nurturing environment for remembering, in which we can reexperience the pain of our own distinctive brokenness, be angry, and begin to grieve over our brokenheartedness, we remain lost to ourselves and each other, cut off from the grace that gives us life.

Institutions within patriarchal structures socialize individuals for conformity to the culture and build character in us through repression and denial. They seldom seek to nurture personal memory and self-understanding. Little time, resources, and space exist in our competitive, goal-oriented culture for profound memory, either in providing the personal time such memory requires or in creating a safe environment for the surfacing of intense pain. While the family has the potential for providing an environment that nurtures self-acceptance, doing so pits it against the socialization expected in a male-dominant culture. The church has encouraged feeling by analogy, as believers are encouraged to mourn the death of Jesus, to be outraged over the sinfulness of "man," and to seek redemption through the suffering of another. The images of the church have the potential to lead us back to our own memory and to empower our self-acceptance, but because images are multifaceted, they are seldom interpreted in healing or liberating ways. In addition, patriarchal ideologies are the dominant perspective of the tradition, its images, theology, and texts.

The Character of Being Human

We begin to heal, in remembrance and forgiveness, by allowing anger to surface, by reconnecting to our deepest, most passionate feelings, feelings grounded in the rich complexities of our full embodied experience, and by actively reclaiming memory, memory grounded in our relationships. In consciousness-raising groups and other feminist contexts, the hearing of each person into her own speech, a process Nelle Morton describes in *The Journey Is Home*, can become a powerful tool of memory and connection. As Morton reports from her experiences, when the empathetic, receptive listening of others allows a woman to tell her own story of suffering fully from beginning to end, that woman is heard into her own liberating speech. My own experiences in such contexts and reports from friends have made me acutely aware of both the pain and healing power of honest memory. Memory that emerges from the heart of ourselves binds us to the suffering of others and provides us the routes to empowerment and self-acceptance. Such memory also makes us hungry for collective memory, for the stories of our own people, and of the truth of the life of the human species.

To act lovingly and ethically, through self-awareness and self-acceptance, does not mean the conquest of our urges and separation from our bodies to gain self-control. To act well, we must be willing to listen to our deepest needs, urges, and feelings and to transform ourselves and our world through the healing energy of heart, which is the only energy capable of touching the hearts of others. In remembering heart we gain an embodied self-acceptance that was taken from us; we reclaim our own fragile original grace and through that our truest human character. With such self-acceptance, we are better able to take on the monumental tasks of transforming patriarchy because our strength comes from heart, a centered energy that radiates outward, giving and receiving love. Original grace allows us to acknowledge our own vulnerability. In living through heart, we can begin to love the world, but we no longer need the world to be fused with us to survive, for we live in connection and beyond separation and dependency. We live in the passionate, impassioned, compassionate world of heart, with courage and integrity.

While confirmation from or with the world no longer becomes necessary for a centered self to survive, the restoration of original grace is difficult because we can only come into flower with connections to other self-accepting selves. This relationality is the terrifying and redemptive grace of the character of being human. Living with self-acceptance, we begin a similar process for other selves. In our fragile interdependence we are powerful. With the arrival of self-acceptance, a new sense of power emerges, one that does not require status and control of others and that does not require using the power of others.

·2·

The Heart of Erotic Power:
The Incarnation of Divine Love

Power is a basic human reality because we are related to each other. However, our conventional understandings of power are colored by our experiences of life in societies of male dominance. From those experiences we come to believe that power is hierarchical and is demonstrated by dominance, by status, by authority, and by control over people, nature, and things. This may be the power we know, but it is not the power we were born with.

The fundamental power of life, born into us, heals, makes whole, empowers, and liberates. Its manifold forms create and emerge from heart, that graceful, passionate mystery at the center of ourselves and each other. This power heals brokenheartedness and gives courage to the fainthearted. It is the feminist Eros, what I call erotic power. Haunani-Kay Trask in *Eros and Power* discusses this union of power with Eros.

> The feminist Eros encompasses the "life force," the unique human energy which springs from the desire for existence with meaning, for a consciousness informed by feeling, for experience that integrates the sensual and the rational, the spiritual and the political. In the feminist vision, Eros is both love *and* power.[1]

Trask ties Eros closely to the bonds formed in early childhood which affect our feelings of sexuality and our relationship to the body as problem or as resource for relationships. The repression of Eros emerges with misogyny, hate of the female as symbol of Eros, the displacement of Eros onto women, and the denial of Eros through aggression against women and alienation from intimacy. Whether women work or not in the public sphere, their relational, nurturant abilities and their erotic potential are the key to their cultural value. In tying love and intimacy to aggression, possession, and domination, societies of male dominance make erotic passion abusive through male symbolic, legal, imagistic, and sexual control over women's bodies. In our male-dominant society Eros is often equivalent to lust or sexuality. This confusion may come from the lack of intimacy accessible to males so that one of the few forms of embodied intimacy available to men is sexual. But the feminist Eros, especially as found in works by Susan Griffin, Audre Lorde, and Adrienne Rich, is far more than sexuality, passion, or an intellectual or spiritual quest for ideal beauty. Feminist Eros is grounded in the relational lives of women and in a critical, self-aware consciousness that unites the psychological and political spheres of life, binding love with power. In addition, Eros involves an appreciation of concrete, embodied beauty and a sense of the tenuousness and fluidity of life. Eros is a sensuous, transformative whole-making wisdom that emerges with the subjective engagement of the whole heart in relationships.

Erotic power is the power of our primal interrelatedness. Erotic power, as it creates and connects hearts, involves the whole person in relationships of self-awareness, vulnerability, openness, and caring. Common understandings of power as dominance and the ability to have one's way—as volitional self-assertion—posit power as causality: the more direct causality, the more power a self possesses. However, erotic power as an ontic category, that is, as a fundamentally ultimate reality in human existence, is a more inclusive and accurate understanding of the dynamics of power within which dominance and willful assertion can be explained. Power as a causal concept is better understood when set into the ontic framework of erotic power as the most inclusive principle of human existence. Hence all other forms of power emerge from the reality of erotic power.

Instead of turning to those who are perceived as strong in order to understand power, this chapter will largely examine the most vulnerable and least conventionally powerful members of society, children, to understand our views of and needs for power. Often studying the most obvious aspects of a social system, especially the most visible or hierarchically powerful parts, leads to a distorted view of the whole. In using the feminist principles of relationship and reversal, I am exploring what we can know about power by examining those perceived as powerless and how the powerful appear from the perspective of those exploited by their power. In systems of power as dominance, those who are powerful have the least access to seeing the whole and, therefore, have the most distorted picture of reality. Looking at power differently gives us a more complete picture of its dynamics and drawbacks. Feminist studies of power examine it from the perspective of those oppressed by it.

The Powerlessness of Dominance

The earliest childhood task is to make order out of the chaos of immediate perceptions so that the world begins to make sense and to respond to intentional acts. A child requires a validating presence and the agreement of others—people it can trust for their wisdom and affectionate support so it can grow toward its own wisdom and generosity. If a child's relationships do not make its acts of receptivity and accommodation worthwhile, it either develops a stronger need for willful assertion into its world or it stays too dependent. The need to dominate or be dominated is the reactive stance of a fearful, defensive self, rather than the centered activity of a confident self. While not limited to masculine identity in our society, a strongly ego-bounded, dominating identity is more characteristic of males. Such a power orientation is crucial to the maintenance of male dominance.

The stereotypical masculine self sees power as a commodity that he increases and uses, which is consistent with the more ego-bounded self discussed in chapter 1. He tries to draw more power over and against others who threaten his supply of power. The quest for dominance involves an ascending thrust toward a transcendental aim, a need to rise and narrow upward toward a hierarchical peak of strength from which all else can be controlled. Stereotypical masculine power is manifested in the self through dominance and aggression. Inequality in relationships is perceived as a permanent state in which power cements status and subordination. The possession of such power is the primary measure of self-worth in the public arenas of our society.

Males see intimate involvement with others as a qualification of power and identity. Strength is the ability to control and hold things external to the self. Power especially associated with male gender identity is the power to get one's way, though power can also be seen as the ability to get along with others and the ability to get things done. In *Powers of the Weak* Elizabeth Janeway describes masculine power as "mastery." Mastery involves individual might, heroic stature, "lone suffering that must win, perhaps, a solution born of the mind of a single genius who has achieved a new vision" (p. 254).

Mastery appears lone, the work of a solitary individual, but it is a characteristic produced by the social structures of male dominance. No one person, whether a king, a warrior-hero, a president, a scientist, or a bishop functions without the tacit cooperation of followers, of others who believe in mastery and compete for similar status, and of social systems designed to reinforce hierarchical authority and dependence upon it. Male dominance relies not on the actions of individual men, but on an entire system that cooperates to reinforce dominance in men. Individual efficacy never lies in one person alone, but in the relationships to which individuals belong. Hierarchical power, while appearing individual, actually is supported by the entire system. Even solitary saviors and martyrs who give their lives for others have no power without those who want and believe in their powers.

Belief in authorities and their power is essential to the maintenance of such power hierarchies. Power as dominance implies that power is something within the individual person that causes changes in others. The person must work in a hierarchy of power and utilize power for self-gain or to promote things to which the self gives herself or himself. Power as dominance implies some access to having one's way.

Hierarchical power carries marked instability. The negative side of the quest for supremacy is a virtually unavoidable decline into failure. The fear of loss and forebodings of the inevitability of defeat are inherent in the quest for the power typical of male gender identity in our society. The terms are set as win-lose. Hence the masculine image of a life's journey is often a tragic one, haunted by failure. In addition, power as dominance carries an illusion of self-sufficiency, cutting the masculine self off from the support of companions and peers who may be called upon for help in difficulty. Hence failure is as lonely as success and far more damaging to a self without support.

In "Two Conceptions of Power" Bernard Loomer calls hierarchical power "unilateral power."[2] Loomer asserts that unilateral power presupposes an ego-centered, self-contained person, one who aims at creating the largest determining effect on others while being minimally influenced by the other. Unilateral power is grounded in competing claims for power, in either/or choices and in the assumption that when someone gains power another has less. Others exist ambiguously as means to the enhancement of one's power or as obstacles to the exercise of one's power. A person values herself or himself on the strength of her or his unilateral power. Loomer states:

> In our struggle for greater power it is essential that the other be as restricted as possible, or that the freedom of the other be contained

within the limits of our control—whether the other be another person or group or the forces of nature. We hesitate or refuse to commit ourselves to those people or realities we cannot control. [p. 16]

Within a system of unilateral power, worth is measured by winning more power. Those with less power have less claim upon life and resources. To keep the threat of other powers under control, the powerful must overinflate their possession of unilateral power. The more one appears to have power, the more value and respect one is accorded.

Loomer notes that repression of aspects of the self that threaten its control and independence are essential to the maintenance of unilateral power. Those capacities and concerns that enhance the specialized interests of unilateral power are abstracted from a full and complete relationship with the self. Similarly, relationships with others and the world focus on abstracting those elements relevant to the purpose of unilateral power.

> Our interest in others is highly selective. . . . we . . . shape ourselves in accordance with our own ethical projections, and thereby maintain both our independence and the feeling of self-determination that accompanies our sense of controlling power. . . . the abstractive character of unilateral power . . . breeds an insensitivity to the presence of the other. [pp. 17–18]

Loomer and Janeway contend that this conception of power has controlled the Western historical experience. Political, military, social, economic, ethical, and theological systems all presuppose unilateral power as dominance. "It is rigorously operative in certain embodiments of leadership as well as in the relations between the sexes" (Loomer, p. 19).

This power orientation begins in family relationships in which dominance is a component. In families in which members are, through control, too fused and parents are unable to see their children as separate from themselves, several reactions ensue. Persons will believe other persons "cause" their behavior and will be unable to see their reactions as their own. Since such relationships are emotionally highly charged, children may react by rebellion and rejection, which in actuality maintains the fusion because each person will continue to see her or his behavior and reactions as "caused" by the others. Hence illusions of narrow, direct causality are maintained.

Fusion is not intimacy and connection, but the antithesis of connection. Fused relationships operate by the deception that two selves are one, that one self can cause the feelings and reactions of others. Such fusion pulls selves off-center. Each self believes the other must be a certain way for it to feel secure. Hence much anger is focused on changing the other, rather than on taking care of the self. The lack of separate selves results in a loss of connection. The distinctive, unique self of the other is not experienced clearly. Because fused relationships are part of interlocked social systems, any change in one part impacts the whole. In that sense, interactions "cause" reactions, but how individuals react to events is not directly caused, in linear fashion, by any particular behavior.[3] Control, domination, and authority in fused relationships are important because the need for self-protection through external structures is part of the systemically fused nature of the relationships.

The Dependency of Powerlessness

Women in patriarchy find themselves on the downside of power hierarchies. They understand power somewhat differently from men, which is consistent with the typical split between the female domestic and male public sphere in male-dominant industrial societies. Females view power as nurturing others. In giving themselves to others to facilitate and empower their growth, females feel powerful. Fusion with others is seen as an aspect of self realization. The feminine view of power is grounded in generosity, empathy, yielding, and relinquishment. This power is important to the domestic task of child-rearing and it does not interfere with the male need to dominate. Instead the feminine self, in feeling powerful by serving others, tends to relinquish a sense of distinctive self. Hence self-esteem becomes lodged in the ability to deny or suppress the self's desires and to cause change in others as extensions of the self.

One of the difficulties in feminine power is its absence in the public sector. While a traditional female may feel powerful in her own sphere through her nurturing activities, her sense of self-esteem and powerfulness do not transfer into the public, male-dominated sector of our society. How a female understands and uses power is directly tied to her life context and the persons with whom she interacts. In a system of domination, in which her sense of powerfulness does not mesh with the dominant system, one female response is self-abnegation and surrender. Hence the lack of a validating presence in childhood results not only in a willful assertion but also in its opposite extreme, dependency. Dependency and guilt, with their accompanying depression, tend to be more characteristic of traditionally feminine power orientations.

In dealing with those whom females perceive as more unilaterally powerful, females tend to relinquish a sense of powerfulness and to hide themselves behind passivity or indirect action. In doing so, they do not give up the need to have their way. Instead they resort to manipulation and indirect modes of activity such as seduction, flattery, helplessness, or control of information, which are ways to accomplish what they want while allowing the other to believe he or she has acted according to his or her own wishes. Through such activity causality becomes tangled and confused. Manipulation causes change indirectly. On the surface, the object of power appears to be the direct cause of the change. In manipulation, the use of rewards power, referent power, and information power are more characteristic ways to achieve goals. The feminine view sees power as the ability to get along with others, which often involves hiding direct action through covert manipulations.

Even when women use such forms of power, their personal objectives may often differ from men's. Instead of wanting to impose their will on others to keep them outside the self and controllable, women seek to push for greater interaction and fusion with others and a sense of importance by participation in their lives. Given the extent to which women and their accomplishments are made invisible in male-dominant cultures, I think, some of the time, at least, that women use covert operations as a way to involve themselves in others' lives without arousing the hostility that more direct and confrontive measures used by men arouse when women use them.

Women who move into the male spheres of public activity tend to assume a masculine orientation to power. Anne Wilson Schaef, in her discussions with professional women found that, while women could be very successful at operating by the rules of male systems of power, they often saw themselves as impostors taking on external roles. They felt deeply ambivalent about functioning with such attitudes toward others. Perhaps because females experience the downside of hierarchical power relationships, they tend to be suspicious about the excess possession and use of dominance. Females are more likely to shun unilateral power for its own sake and to see the desire for power as negative.

The masculine and feminine views of power remain split into two sides of a dualism as polarized opposites. The two views of power depend on each other in a gender-stratified system of dominance and submission. Exploiter male and exploited female go hand in hand, just as powerful, controlling parent and abused child fit a system of hierarchical power. In patriarchal systems, the feminine view of power hardly seems like power at all, but appears to be weakness. Yet the illusion of polarization hides the similarity of the two views. While the male seeks to dominate those with less power, he is expected to sacrifice himself to God, country, or company. Hence, while self-sacrifice and martyrdom seem more feminine, being exploited is expected of men for the sake of higher authority. Escape from exploitation must be through attainment of higher authority, a more typically masculine aspiration, or through protection sought from it, a more typically feminine approach. In addition, both male domination and female dependency require the suppression of the self's own feelings.

The difficulty in fused relationships, either in provoking reactions of rebellion and separation, like an angry, bossy response, or in reactions of dependency and need, like a helpless, depressive response, is that neither reaction produces healthy, self-affirming intimacy. Hence dominance or dependency does not allow self-acceptance or intimacy because the underlying fusion prohibits a clear sense of self.

The orientation toward dominance—to be controlled or to control—is the reaction to an abusive childhood. The need for personal authority, control, and dominance, as well as an inability to assert oneself against abusive treatment and demands for self-sacrifice, are symptomatic of wounded selves and are defensive reactions to fear. The more control and punishment oriented a parent, the more children will "behave" only when they fear a higher, punitive authority, and the more adults, so raised, will seek self-protection through authority or powerful others. In addition, such adults will protect authority from criticism and seek to educate all those under their control to respect authority. Thus authority comes to replace self-love and a sense of personal worth.

Power as control manifests itself in interpersonal and intrapersonal dimensions. The damaged inner psychic world—the broken heart—is mirrored in external behavior. The fearful person behaves well through self-control over internal feelings that conflict with "right" behavior. She or he has internalized a fused, controlling relationship. Thus the broken-hearted self denies its own pain by using control over feelings. The fearful self uses will to suppress a broken heart. Alice Miller rejects this model of mastery as the ideal, moral, loving person. In *For Your Own Good* she states:

> Morality and performance of duty are artificial measures that become necessary when something essential is lacking. The more successfully a

person was denied access to his or her feelings in childhood, the larger the arsenal of intellectual weapons and the supply of moral prostheses has to be, because morality and a sense of duty are not sources of strength or fruitful soil for genuine affection...I am inclined to see courage, integrity, and a capacity for love not as "virtues," not as moral categories, but as the consequences of a benign fate.[4]

The need for control of self and others that Miller describes is based on a failure to develop confident self-acceptance. Miller acknowledges the necessity for control when self-love is buried and the damaged self needs grounding. She asserts, however, that control and dominance are weaker and less reliable than that strength which comes from a centered self—a heartfelt self, opening to the world and embracing a full range of inner feelings. This open, interactive, self-expressiveness is different from either the need to impose our will upon the world or the need to lose ourselves in the feelings and needs of others. It is the root of intimacy and connection, and springs from and enhances erotic power.

Fused relationships begin in the family, but once they are internalized, fusion extends itself into social systems. Power is an important dimension of interpersonal and intergroup relationships. In our society persons feel present, alive, and sustained in the world through the power to influence and participate in shaping their world. Power is essential to self-esteem, to freedom, and to well-being. But we tend to think of power, deterministically and causally, as a commodity owned and used by the self for its purposes. While individuals differ in their motives for seeking power—some seek it for itself; others seek it as a means to feeling personally valuable; some even try to avoid certain forms of it as burdensome—it is a crucial dimension of existence.

Both dominance and compliance confuse personal power with positional power.[5] Positional power has to do with our status in social relationships and the extent to which our interpersonal world has emphasized control. The more a social structure functions by control, the more it produces people preoccupied with power based on status. Males seek to gain greater dominance and status. Females use indirect power to align themselves with someone who possesses positional power because they perceive themselves as powerless in male systems. When power is seen as something possessed by an individual who uses it causally, connecting power will be thought to diminish those involved because vulnerability and connectedness will be seen as threats to, rather than as enhancements of selves.

Personal power grows out of erotic power through self-awareness and self-affirmation. It comes when we live by heart and is the individual aspect of erotic power. We experience our feelings, thoughts, and responses to the world as distinctive and unique to ourselves. Through that experience of heart we are able to act in ways that affirm ourselves without hurting others and to find and create environments that enhance our lives and the lives of others. The paradox of personal power is its relational base. We can only become self-aware and self-accepting through relationships that cocreate us, and the maintenance of nonharmful environments requires sustained, nurturing relationships. Self-acceptance, as an ongoing, lifelong process, is possible only through our openness to others and their presence. In the personal awareness of self-in-relationships, we are empowered to respond and act toward intimacy instead of dependency and toward greater openness and self-affirmation instead of self-sacrifice.

Power is a psychological, social, political, and theological issue. As a theological concept, power has been central to any discussion of divine efficacy. Our understandings of power impact what we believe about the worth and purpose of life and about the nature of divine reality.

In moving to a nondualistic relational understanding of power, a number of process thinkers—those who believe that relationship and change are ultimate principles of reality—have attempted to replace coercive power with persuasive power. This is an important move away from control and from religious discussions of power as coercive or as the benign paternalistic interactions of God with the world. However, much of the time they discuss how much power God has, as opposed to how much the world and its creatures have in actualizing their various purposes. While persuasion suggests mutuality and egalitarianism, it continues to connote the actor who may intentionally affect another's behavior through an effective use of the power she or he possesses. Persuasion is the most reliable form of power from the standpoint of the possessor because it runs the least risk of arousing opposition from the power subject. Nonetheless, persuasion still connotes possession of power by an actor who attempts to get his or her own way. We must move from seeing power as a commodity possessed by a self toward seeing it as the bonds which create and sustain, and are recreated and sustained by relational selves.

Feminist research on gender difference and power has raised serious question about androcentrism in our society's perceptions of power and the destructive and oppressive implications of such perceptions. Institutions of male dominance that oppress women and divide society into gender-linked roles and value systems produce the difficulty we face because they produce the differing views of power. In examining the social structures that are characteristic of male-dominant societies, feminists look at power from below and hold under scrutiny every aspect of power relationships. Male-dominant systems tend to assume that androcentric views of reality are all-inclusive. Feminists claim otherwise, as do an increasing number of thinkers who re-vision reality in nondualistic terms. Relativity physics has called into question the traditional subject-object dichotomy of Western science. Buddhism, while having a history of misogyny and androcentrism, has been examined by feminists such as Joanna Macy and Rita Gross for its importance to a nondualistic vision of reality. Process thinkers like Charles Hartshorne, John Cobb, and Bernard Meland present theologies based in a nondualistic world view. In inflicting gender divisions on its members, our society cuts off those who work in public power spheres from an understanding of power that is crucial to the survival of the human species.

To a greater or lesser extent, we live in societies dominated by the crushing of heart, by heart dis-ease. That has been our fate. Our fate has also been to live ambivalently with brokenheartedness and with possibilities for healing and wholeness through the work of erotic power.

The Heart of the Matter

Family relationships can nurture heart. The first awarenesses of an infant are the connection between self and other and the necessity of expressing its needs and having them satisfied. Intimacy grows through a highly interactive process of mutual recognition and validation from significant others. The interaction between a child's developing self and its world happens across an intermediary space, the space of heart in which creativity through connection occurs. It is the space of play, a personal space for erotic power. Children play with elements of their environment and relationships to create an orderly, reliable world inside themselves. Their playing creates an inner object world, the resources of images with which they recreate personal mythic versions of reality. But to create versions that are both expressions of their own unique selves and reliably accurate reflections of their world, children must be able to trust their environment as they maintain the precarious and exciting tension between self and world.

Children's worlds of internalized objects begin to serve dreams and feelings so that playing moves from isolated self-playing to shared playing to the creativity of shared cultural experiences. Children internalize external objectsthat become symbols of their inner and outer worlds. The play space is neither totally intrapsychic nor external. Transitional play space is the exciting interweaving of subjective feeling and objective observation. Play is intermediate between the self and its capacity to share in a larger culture of persons and symbols.

In *Playing and Reality* Donald Winnicott discusses the ultimate importance of play for the development of healthy persons.[6] He describes the function of psychotherapy as two persons playing together. When a person is unable to play, the task of the therapist is to return the person to playing. Play is not frivolous or trivial, but life-sustaining. It is the basis of freedom, creativity, and spontaneity.

When the outer world of the self is not loving, supportive, and reliable enough, the inner self must become rigid to protect its need to create a coherent world. The centered, focused energy of erotic power that plays with the world becomes hidden. Without support, the self becomes extremely isolated, enraged, afraid to connect with reality, basing itself in protective, untrue pictures of life. Play is lost, and the self's ability to distinguish between inner and outer world, between subjectivity and objectivity, is attenuated. Marginalized from intimacy with the world, such selves seek to assert control over the world or to give in as victims of it. Causality begins to be seen as direct and narrow, as deterministic. In this narrowing of freedom, gender identity and power fall into polarized sides of self-deceptive, fused relationships: in masculine identity by the attempt to shape the world according to the isolated self; in feminine identity by the surrender of self to the external world. Both result from control.

Erotic power denied and crushed produces dominance and control. Healing the wounded heart restores openings for the flowering of erotic power through the self-accepting, creative self. A healthy child lives in and through heart. The child's power is the graceful capacity to play and to cocreate self and world. As Elizabeth Janeway states,

> In order to create a secure identity, the child invents a world. . . . Unless we make and match interior reality with what we are assured is out there, we cannot function in either place. The deepest understanding of power and its uses is woven into the construction of a self, and this construction can take place only through the mediation of others, in established relationships. . . . Power can be properly defined only as a relationship between or among human beings. [pp. 47—48]

Play links self and world. Through playing the heart heals, connects, and creates. The relational play space itself is the locus of erotic power, as that space exists between the individual and her or his world. Erotic power is recreated and sustained through the playful heart as a lifelong adventure. As the relational source of our vulnerability and connectedness to the world through heart, erotic power cannot be possessed. Erotic power creates and sustains connectedness—intimacy, generosity, and interdependence.

The difficulty of understanding power as relational bonds is lodged partly in the Western tendency to focus on sensory perception as the only reliable, measurable knowledge. Through such knowledge, things are known externally to us, especially in unilateral, causal relationships that are objectifiable. Sensory perception is an important way we know our world, but not our inner selves. The inner physical feelings of our body and the emotions we know inside our bodies are not told to us through our five senses. The knowledge of ourselves stored in our memory and the messages sent to us in dreams come from a world not tied in any immediate way to our senses. Yet these are important, subjective forms of knowing. They are, as it were, knowing by heart.

Erotic power involves inner and outer worlds in a knowing that is multilayered and a causality that is multilateral and intertwined. For example, if I listen to a friend tell the story of a childhood molestation, her pain communicates itself vividly to me. But the pain I experience, triggered by hers, emerges from within me. It is not her pain, though it mirrors hers and enables me to take her pain into me. If I am oblivious to my own feelings and confuse mine with hers, I will experience my own pain through hers, making her uniqueness invisible. If I refuse my own feelings because I fear my own pain, my impassivity or my deflecting her pain by making it abstract or universal will reduce her presence to me. Maintaining my self-awareness, which allows my openness to her, allows me to respond in my own unique, creative way to her pain. Our empowerment comes not in her pain or in mine but in the space where the two meet inside us and between us. In that meeting, in the feelings underneath the speaking and listening, we are empowered to care and to heal. When I experience my own empowerment through connection, I know power emerges from my relationships.

Bernard Loomer calls the power to sustain mutually internal relationships "relational power." He asserts that the depth to which we are open and remain committed to relationships is the extent of our power. In his view, to exclude others from our world of meaning and concern is to act out of powerlessness and fear. To exist within permanently hierarchical relationships is to limit the extent to which we can receive and give in relationships. And the final source of any power is through mutually internal relationships.

"Relation" in the internal sense is a way of speaking of the presence of others in our own being. It is the peculiar destiny of process/relational thought to have transformed this commonplace but deep-seated observation into a metaphysical first principle. [p. 22]

The strength of Loomer's insight is its inclusivity; even controlling power draws its life from relationships rather than from an isolated self. The perception of those relationships and the consequences of such perceptions affect self-identity. Unilateral power creates individuals who lack strength and stature because they are psychically small and brittle. Those who live by unilateral power do not acknowledge their dependence upon those they control and label as weak even though they depend upon the "weak" for survival. Hence relationships within unilateral power are attenuated because of their self-deception.

If power always means the exercising of influence and control, and if receiving always means weakness and a lack of power, then a creative and strong love that comprises a mutual giving and receiving is not possible. [p. 21]

Loomer's insights into power are paralleled in Janeway's thesis on the powers of the weak. While accepting the traditional definition of the weak as an acknowledgement of their perceived status by those in positions of authority, Janeway believes this idea of weakness is false. For all power is the product of relationships, whether or not such interdependence is acknowledged. Janeway seeks to redefine power along nonpolarized, nondualistic lines. She believes the so-called weak can transform society by bonding together and by calling into question dominant forms of thought, especially about power. The weak have an untapped *latent* power, binding them to the "strong," that, when understood, transforms our understanding of power. Janeway criticizes the analytical view of power which tends to focus on the powerful—the view from above, as it were.

To be content with this view alone is to agree that power belongs to the powerful as an attribute or possession, a kind of magic wand that compels obedience. Such an appraisal leaves out the deeply grounded relatedness in which new human creatures find their own identities through the intervention of others, whose presence mediates and interprets the whole ground of reality. [p. 21]

Loomer and Janeway shift our understanding of power away from something any one individual or group possesses alone. They urge us to see it as something created by relationships. In doing so, we can begin to see power in whole events and interactions.

All powers, including the most destructive, depend on relationships. But once this insight begins to sink in, how we interact with each other becomes a far more crucial question. For if we choose some element of domination, no matter how benevolent, we reduce the presence of the other in the relationship, and thereby diminish the creativity of connection and the wonder and mystery of erotic power.

Alfred North Whitehead and Charles Hartshorne have argued that the key to human awareness and action is *experience*, experience understood in its integrating complexity. Hence how we perceive, understand, and organize the events of our lives has a great deal to do with our behavior. As Hartshorne states in *The Logic of Perfection*:

> While experience is certainly influenced by its data (which are its only conditions), it seems evident that it can never be wholly determined by them. A "creative synthesis" is required, without which the experience would be merely the given data over again.[7]

Erotic power is the energy that produces creative synthesis, and is enhanced by the relationships that emerge from creative synthesis. It produces not fusion and control, but connectedness. While various forms of dominance exist in society, if we can begin to experience them differently, we will begin to break down the damaging power hierarchies that destroy heart. We can then begin to see power as the fluid product of a highly interactive process that begins with birth and buoys us throughout life. Erotic power emerges in and maintains the play space allowing the engagement of our whole being and world of experience. Such a view of power may seem new, but it, in fact, is a more primal awareness of life that taps the energy sources of our earliest beginnings when, as children, we were most vulnerable and needed to connect to others. The childhood birth of play and the rebirth of heart lead us into the many realms of erotic power.

Erotic power integrates all aspects of the self, making us whole. Erotic power grounds the concreteness of our experiences of empathy, passion, creativity, sensuality, and beauty. Erotic power resides in the matrices of our connectedness to self, to the body, to others, and to the world. Through it we experience in the richness of our lives—in our bodies, psyches, and spirits—the flowering of ourselves and our worlds. Erotic power in human life has been richly articulated by several feminist theorists, including those whose works are briefly discussed below.

Unlike agape, which is often defined as a disinterested, or objective form of love, most exemplified in the dispassionate divine love, Eros connotes intimacy through the subjective engagement of the whole self in a relationship. It is sometimes confused with lust, or sexuality. Trask's analysis in *Eros and Power* of Freud and Marcuse suggests that patriarchy under capitalism turns Eros into sexual domination by the repression of sex instincts through childhood and puberty, "during which time the body is progressively desexualized by parents and other authorities" [p. 9].

This process submits women to male dominance as the object of projections of Eros. Hence women are the core of the repression of sexuality.

This repression of sexuality brings people into line with the demands of an acquisitive, aggressive society prescribing heterosexual possession and prohibiting spontaneous liaisons and nongenital sex as "*immoral* or *unnatural*." The end result of this repression is an alteration of sexuality from an expressive aspect of the entire person into a specialized function,

> a means to an end, . . . a desexualization of the body for the fulfillment
> of the performance principle, that is, alienated labor. . . . the "toneless"
> pleasure principle is subjugated to the performance principle [which]
> decrees an acquisitive, aggressive ego. [Trask, pp. 9–10]

Trask sees the feminist articulation of Eros as moving well beyond the identification of passion and love with genital sexuality to a sense of the body and a power that cherishes life in its multiplicities of feelings and forms.

In "Uses of the Erotic: The Erotic as Power," Audre Lorde, describes the erotic as the ability to feel our deepest passions in all aspects of our lives as the root of our lives' deepest meanings.[8] The life force behind the creative, empowering energy of our lives is the erotic. The erotic bridges the passions of our lives by a sensual span of physical, emotional, psychic, mental, and spiritual elements.

The erotic cannot be felt secondhand; it can only be felt through our own unique presence and the presence of others to us. The erotic underlies all levels of experience, openly and fearlessly, with intense joy. As we feel deeply the complex, many dimensions of ourselves, we begin to want the joy that we know emerges through the erotic. We begin to examine our lives for the excellence and fulfillment we glimpse in erotic power. We are empowered to refuse the convenient, shoddy, conventional, and safe. The erotic compels us to be hungry for justice at our very depths because we are response-able. We are able to reject what makes us numb to the suffering and self-hate of others. Acts against oppression become essential to ourselves, empowered from our energized centers. Through the erotic as power we become less willing to accept powerlessness, despair, depression, and self-denial. The erotic is what binds and gives life and hope. It is the energy of all relationship and it connects us to our embodied selves. The empathetic sharing of any pursuit with another person helps us understand what is not shared. Hence differences become less threatening as we are empowered to affirm all persons in our lives, and to see through the faint, fearful, broken heart of patriarchy.

In *Pornography and Silence* Susan Griffin describes Eros as the basic yearning for others and for self-discovery. Our deepest selves—our hearts—seek the intimate relationships toward which Eros lures us. To be in relationship with a changing world is to recognize, according to Griffin, that we are constantly changing. To choose domination and isolation is to deny Eros. However, Griffin acknowledges that the surrender to such a process is not an easy one. For she is aware of the damage we all carry. Surrender means recognizing that we are fragile and interdependent, subject to forces outside ourselves. To be such open selves is to be easily damaged, yet to be so is essential to healthy psychic survival. The reunion inside us of nature, of desire, of sensuality, of change, of darkness, of death, of vulnerability, of receptivity, and of the child in us are, for Griffin, the only way to become whole.

All power emerges from erotic power either, in life-giving form, from our acknowledgment of it and our ability to live in that understanding or, in destructive form, from the brokenheartedness that refuses to understand it. The erotic is the basis of being itself as the power of relationship, and all existence comes to be by virtue of connectedness, from atoms to the cosmos. Erotic power is the fundamental power of existence-as-a-relational-process. Metaphysically, nothing can exist without the connections that make it what it continues to become through space and time. Connection is the basic power of all existence, the root of life. The power of being/becoming is erotic power. Erotic power leads us, through the human heart, toward life-giving cocreating.

Erotic power, unlike control, domination, or authority (which we believe, self-deceptively, we can possess), cannot be fixed or clung to because it cannot be controlled, won, possessed, or created. We are born in it as we are born in the physical structures of the universe. Erotic power is the very foundation of life and the source of energy for human selves that compels us to search for the whole of life. This power affirms, creates, and is recreated in human existence by heart. As the foundation of heart, erotic power compels us toward compassion, collective action, integration, self-acceptance, and self-reflective memory in our critical recollection of the past.

But as brokenheartedness poignantly reveals, our patriarchal society can cut us off from the life-giving power of the erotic. Patriarchal ideologies require that we split off parts of ourselves so that we may be self-righteously "correct" and good, no matter what the cause—feminism, Christianity, civil rights, liberation, and so on. Such a self-righteous split divides self and world so that psychological self-examination and personal responsibility are set against the political realities of institutionalized oppression. The personal and political—the therapeutic and ethical—are sharply divided. Such polarization tends to set distinctions and differences as oppositions, heightening conflict while making it difficult for us to recognize or integrate conflict.

In "The Way of All Ideology" Susan Griffin calls for us to relearn thinking.[9] Our reflection must explore self and world with a desire to integrate. Without the integration of sensation, feeling, and thinking, our dialogues with each other and the shape of our efforts toward liberation will be imprisoned behind ideologies that erase our sometimes contradictory and paradoxical experiences. She suggests that in both the psychological and political quests for understanding are hope for changing the world for the better and a profound acknowledgement of our own woundedness and the damaged state of the world. Griffin sees in both perspectives a passionate desire to heal suffering and a forgiving vision of the world. In the desire to understand and to rejoin what is broken, they seek for the whole.

> And this desire to know is perhaps finally a way to loving. For the desire to know deeply all that is, as part of our outrage over injustice and suffering, accepts the truth, the whole and compassionate being. [p. 660]

The Heart of the Universe

Out of our acceptance of the whole and compassionate being, new awarenesses emerge that lead us to a knowing from the heart that transforms worlds. Elizabeth Janeway speaks of messages from the self's interior, of dream, fantasy, and myth—messages of feeling in which the realm of play becomes magic in its transformative capacity. In this realm, images well up from experience and emotional need and communicate what is puzzling, frightening, or challenging and what has not been satisfied by events in the outer world.

> Dreams give us happy endings to desires when the world won't; and sometimes they also hint slyly why it is that the world refuses to grant our wishes. Thus they provide practice for ordering and reordering the inner images of reality. [p. 66]

In so-called primitive societies, trances are important as a source of healing and wisdom. In trances spirits which dwell in the concrete world of reality—ancestral spirits, the recently dead, nature deities, tricksters, and other cosmic powers that touch life—can be called upon for messages of wisdom, healing, and foresight. The messages of shamanistic trances are often playfully symbolic, vague, and allusive, requiring both intense focused concentration by the medium and wise interpretation. The shift from trance to dream, from a more conscious awareness of the magic of the play space and memory, to a more unconscious state may represent a shift from egalitarian societies with horizontal cosmologies to male-dominant societies with vertical cosmologies and more distant, alienated gods. In "Patriarchal Revolution in Ancient Japan" Robert Ellwood argues that the ancient shamaness trance spirituality of prepatriarchal Japan was replaced with a male priest-centered religion in which gods sent messages in dreams.[10] Marjorie Shostak in *Nisa* and Richard Katz in *Boiling Energy: Community Healing Among the Kalahari Kung* describe the egalitarian healing trances of the !Kung, trances which bind and heal the entire community. But our society has lost its capacity to listen to trances or dreams.[11]

Our technocratic, rationally oriented society has great difficulty dealing with dreams and the shamanistic magic of mythic images, except to relegate them to fiercely rational psychological analysis, or to images as art. In rejecting anything that might smack of supernaturalism, we draw our truth concepts predominantly from cognitive awareness. The literalism and reductionism of scientific thinking and its reliance on objective truth results in a one-to-one fusion of self and world, cause and effect, predictability and control. The self disappears into its objective observation of objects and pretends it has removed itself. This outmoded but still common concept of objectivity in Western thought assumes that a neutral place exists from which an observer, whose presence does not interfere with the event taking place, can tell what "really" occurred. This assumption of objectivity grounds the scientific method and is used to subordinate ideas that overtly take an advocacy position. This myth of objectivity has been challenged in Marxist, feminist, and process thought and by relativity physics.

Many cultures, especially those that the intellectual West has called "primitive," and that are more relationally oriented, delve far deeper into the subjective realms of dream and magic and give these realms external reality. Awake, we ignore the richness of subjective connections to others and the play space provided by multivalent images because we tend toward logical linearity. Hence we lose connections to our own creative insights. Yet, as Janeway reminds us, "each of us civilized human beings has to expect to spend some hours of every day in a world where emotional linkage operates with vivid actuality" (p. 80).

The distinction between the imaginative, interactive play space of myths, feelings, and dreams and the linear, cognitive orientation of our technocratic culture can also be seen in the difference in orientation to reality between oral and literate cultures, a difference that can be discerned in the development from foraging societies to advanced agrarian empires. Gerda Lerner notes the political implications of the development of writing in agrarian societies as it allowed greater control for an elite class and a different orientation to time and space. Writing strengthened the leadership of elite classes by giving them greater control over governance and sacred knowledge. The gradual cultural shifts involved in writing moved people toward a worship of the power of abstraction, which can become a means of controlling illiterate masses, and of a more linear orientation to time and a visual orientation to space. Through abstraction the observable facts of female reproduction can be transmuted into a symbolic creativity of the word to the concept of the "creative spirit of the universe." Without such a move, exclusive monotheism is impossible. With such a move, large numbers of people can be persuaded to imagine and follow an abstract, more unilateral orientation to reality, as a writer can be detached from social context and exercise a great deal of control over composition and idea.

In *The Oral and Written Gospel*, a discussion of oral culture and written canon, Werner Kelber claims that in oral cultures people have access to the same memory capacities as their leaders and storytellers.[12] The people's participation in and cocreation of political and sacred knowledge is well developed. Oral language is personal, holistic in its involvement of persons, and resonant interactively among participants. Sacred knowledge is not made true through its historical reliability, "but on the authority of the speaker and by the reception of the hearer" (p. 71).

While we cannot escape belonging to a literate society, I believe we must pay closer attention to the differences between an oral and a literate orientation to reality. For oral culture allows a multifaceted, flexible orientation to language and reality that is highly interactive, contextual, and transformative. Language carries complex feeling; time is cyclical, constantly doubling back on itself; space is multisensory. We cannot return to oral culture, for we are too thoroughly literate and historical. A more accurate sense of history is an important element in understanding our own patriarchal past. History is the primary way our society has chosen to understand its past. However, the oral roots of human society may be an important dimension of ourselves, our society, and the sacred.

This attention to the oral is especially crucial if we want to understand human memory and spirituality. Attention must be paid to oral roots both in a historical sense and in a psychological sense. The play space of human selves is developed in an early oral environment. Literacy develops out of our earlier oral experiences and the linguistic skills we learn there. Its roots are interpersonal, interactive, cyclical, multisensory, and contextual. Play space becomes attenuated when external control enters the picture. When imagination is too literal, when its creations are understood to correspond one to one with reality, it shrinks. Hence a too cognitive, too literal, and too alienated orientation to reality reduces its spiritual power, its erotic power. The flexibility of oral cultures parallels the capacity to play. This fluid world of play, where the self interacts with its world and creates itself and reality anew, is, I believe, a crucial aspect of the mysterious whirling realm of erotic power.

As the dancing mystery of the sacred, the magic of connection is the confirmation of divine presence in human life. This power affirms, creates, and is recreated by heart. It is the very foundation of our lives and the center of an energy that compels us to search for the whole of life, which is its fullest ongoing incarnation.

Erotic power is incarnate in heart. It binds the life-giving, healing heart of ourselves with each other, if we possess the courage to claim it. For courage itself wells from the heart. And heart enhances erotic power through our connections to others. Searching for connections is the heart's search, the search to heal suffering and brokenness.

Heart lives in erotic power, the power of our loving each other at the depths of our being. In expanding the feminist concept of erotic power to include its sacred dimensions, I am developing its theological implications as the incarnation of divine love. The presence and revelation of erotic power is the divine dimension of human existence. It grows and moves with us as the resilient, flexible vulnerability that reveals our existence in relationship and our cocreation of each other. Erotic power is with us at the origins of our own concrete lives and sustains us lifelong.

In the beginning is the divine Eros, embodied in all being. As the incarnate, life-giving power of the universe, divine erotic power is the Heart of the Universe. In *Omnipotence and Other Theological Mistakes* Charles Hartshorne suggests we move beyond theological analogies of parent-child relationships to the more intimate and accurate analogy of mind and body as descriptive of the divine relationship to the world.[13] But the connection of mind to rationality and logos and its history of dualistic separation from the body limits the usefulness of the mind/body analogy, even when it is explained in the nondualistic, relational terms of process thought. Imagining the divine presence in the world as Heart leads us to a greater sense of the whole of life as sacred.

Seeking for Eros, according to Griffin, leads us to the sacred. We become part of an ineffable ecstasy that binds us to the whirling mystery within ourselves, to the deepest unspeakable mystery of the sacred. But to be open to the creative insights of erotic power, we must be open to connection, to feeling, to sensuality, and to the play spaces of the fullness of experience, to images, dreams, myths, and magic. Janeway recognizes such openness as powerful in its political implications for transforming society.

> To change ourselves, to change relationships, to change the world—all these work together and can't be separated, and all of them will supply us with new data, as we update our chart. . . . I like to imagine . . . a few features dating back to a time when play and poetry and metaphor were not excluded from serious business. . . . let us . . . work toward a map of uncertain prediction connecting to memory, a map of promise, a map of possibility, of an unbounded future that will not be limited by an end. [p. 321]

This unbounded future begins with Eros.

Eros is what Alfred North Whitehead in *Adventures of Ideas* calls the divine incarnation that moves us into the future.[14] He describes Eros as that which urges the human soul to a synthesis of a "new fact which is the Appearance woven out of the old and the new—a compound of reception and anticipation, which in turn passes into the future" (p. 275). In such a process,

Whitehead urges that all human experience, not simply rational, cognitive thinking, be explored for truth. Without Eros—the divine yearning for playful becoming—new unities within the individual cannot emerge for the future.

The spiritual quest is an attunement to the graceful moments of life, according to Bernard Meland in *Fallible Forms and Symbols*. [15] He insists on culture and actual experience as resources for understanding. He criticizes the quest for rational certainty in our culture as that which cuts us away from an attunement to the depth of human experience, an attunement he calls "appreciative awareness." Meland insists *"we live more profoundly than we can think . . .* even when we address ourselves in the profoundest way possible to the issues of our existence" (p. 82).

Meland believes the task of theology is to dwell on the margins of our structures of existence, margins with "an unmanageable depth of grace and freedom that opens into a relational ground" and exceeds the reach of concepts, concepts which become false gods. To create life anew and to relate to a larger world requires receptivity toward the depth of lived experience, which is far more than the technical, critical, and intellectual. Under the guise of knowing, rational thinking can project limited and fallible symbols upon the "more than we can think." For Meland, a sole reliance on reason is divisive and alienating because it demands allegiance to one strain of thought or an ideology. He calls for a more sensitive

> encounter with realities at the edge of our being. . . . In a world of contextual meaning, dissonance takes on the import of qualitative distinctions which, in themselves, carry values to be cherished and sustained. . . . Such dissonance can mean a readiness to live together with differences in the interest of retaining, cherishing, and hopefully participating to some degree in the complexity of meaning and value which these . . . differences offer. [pp. 130, 198]

Meland, like Janeway and Griffin, is calling for religious life to be lived in the play space, in the realm of imaginative open interaction with the world.

Another process thinker, Henry Nelson Wieman develops an extensive argument for the primacy of connection in *The Source of Human Good*. [16] Wieman believes the only reliable basis for absolute good in human existence is relationship. Good is grounded in our deep awareness of others, our willingness to participate in mutual transformation, the expansion of quality, the increase of meaning that comes from increasing connectedness, and the deepening of communion among all who participate in relationship. Because no single person can achieve such good alone, the good that emerges is suprahuman. The good that includes but moves beyond our own individual existence to become sacred emerges from the risks each of us takes to be vulnerable to relationships. Mutual support, intercommunication, and sensitive openness, the only avenues of divine power that create good, require enormous risks.

Wieman argues vehemently that no appeal to eternity or transcendent power can save us. If we cannot develop a faith that makes sense of our most concrete, puzzling, and problematic experiences, we have no redemptive faith. Wieman calls for a radical redirection of human devotion to the deepest sources of our connectedness that generate and recreate ongoing relationships. Hence, like the feminists cited above, Wieman is calling for a demystification of faith. Through it, we can come to understand what leads us to spiritual life.

We are led, according to Wieman, by signs, the shorthand codes that communicate experience and expand our capacity for connection to all that is. Wieman's notion of signs is similar to the idea of play images and to Janeway's map into the future. Signs connect us through our imagination to worlds beyond our immediate apprehension. Signs reveal "the secrets of many hearts" (p. 22). In doing so, signs participate in the life of conscious awareness and take on richer qualitative meanings.

> As these meanings form a network of interconnective events comprehending all that is happening in the world, this universe becomes spiritual. . . . It becomes more deeply and pervasively meaningful. It becomes the house of the human spirit. . . . Events cease to be material things merely and become a language, a prophecy, and a song. [p. 23]

Wieman claims as long as signs remain flexible and move in relationships (they remain playful) and not fixed in final form, they perform their spiritual function. These signs point us to the deepest sources of our connectedness, to heart.

But an open play space can only happen if some element of grace is maintained in a life. We are vulnerable, fragile. The self at times may not be able to open such a space if its world will not help create it. Inner conflicts that paralyze the self indicate brokenheartedness. The conflicts of a broken heart have the potential of ultimate self-destruction, but, as the heart struggles to surface, the destruction can be seen as a sign of the heart's presence.

Similarly, the revolutions and battles of groups of oppressed people to free themselves from tyranny, even when they hurt the oppressed themselves, are clear signs of the presence of the fundamental human need for love and dignity, for right relationships. If we turn deaf ears to such outcries of pain and numb ourselves to such destruction, we will miss important clues to how we can heal such brokenness and reclaim heart.

Reproducing patriarchal family structures and seeing power as the possession of a self or group over and against others raise serious question about sanctifying, in a written canon, such oppressive divine images and theological doctrines. Christian theology has done so, both through almost exclusively masculine symbols such as father, king, lord, and savior and through theological doctrines of omnipotence and divine *apatheia*, judgment, and reason. At times the unconventional use of male-dominant images has shattered their hierarchical hold by a transmutation of the image into its opposite, for example, when the messianic king becomes a servant. However, the doctrine of omnipotence, by connection to such images, has tended to reinforce their hierarchical, controlling aspects. While each of these images conveys something of our understanding of authority, unilateral power, and selfless giving, they are a patriarchal legacy, symbol systems of hierarchical and oppressive societies. And the images have, I believe, reinforced the dynamics of mutuality sustained by paternalism. They have not often brought us to transforming insights that lead to erotic power because they tend to reinforce patriarchal structures of power as dominance and authority and love as obedience.

Christianity is afflicted with a hierarchical view of power that undercuts its understanding of love in its fullest incarnation—that we are all part of one another and cocreate each other at the depths of our being. In recognizing how we have been afflicted with the broken heart of patriarchy, we can begin to see the territories of connection beyond patriarchal powers. Heart is the guide into those new territories; erotic power is the energy of incarnate love.

·3·

The Feminist
Redemption of Christ

The pervasive, profoundly patriarchal elements of Christianity have forced those of us who consider ourselves feminist and Christian to struggle intensely with our faith and our commitments to justice and wholeness. Our decisions to leave or to stay within Christianity are less important than what our struggles have revealed about the oppressive, patriarchal character of so much of Christian history and theology. The feminist vision of healing, wholeness, and spirituality must save Christianity from its patriarchy—if Christian theology is to remain true to its claims that all human beings are created in the divine image, that divine power is love in its fullness, and that the community of divine power is one of justice and peace.

Feminist theological critiques of Christianity make the maintenance of its patriarchal family structures in christology unacceptable. Feminists such as Rosemary Ruether and Mary Daly stand in a long line of iconoclasts such as Freud, Nietzsche, Fromm, and Hartshorne who have attacked the negative impact of denying persons their full humanity through authoritarian and punitive images of divine power.

Alice Miller explains how an abused child needs to respect and protect a nostalgic image of the punitive control-oriented parent, an image that is reflected in theology. Our oppressive, patriarchal doctrines are a result of the abusive treatment of children in a patriarchal culture. To free ourselves of cycles of abuse, we need theologies that reveal the Heart of the Universe.

In looking for christological clues about the presence and work of erotic power, I will be occupied with a theological task. However, my interpretations are indebted to historical research in biblical studies, which has also come increasingly to understand the biblical texts as theological statements. Within the texts I believe we find hints of life-transforming realities based in erotic power, in images both of brokenheartedness and of the healing of heart. The focus of redemption has been traditionally lodged in Jesus as the Christ, reflecting, I believe, an androcentric preoccupation with heroes. Life-giving relational realities were nonetheless present, and they can be discerned in biblical images that lead us toward the reclaiming of heart. Before moving to a discussion of biblical images of erotic power, I will discuss why I do not find christologies that base themselves in Jesus adequate for transforming patriarchy and healing suffering.

Several assumptions guide my search for christological images of erotic power. First, while christology, broadly defined, is the logical explanation of Christian faith claims about divine presence and salvific activity in human life, theological explanations emerge from particular social, historical contexts. Hence abstract, philosophical concepts have political and psychological roots. The convincing quality of any idea lies first in what Whitehead, in *Modes of Thought*, called interest, in the feelings that lie behind a commitment to the search for truth and in the intuitive sense of connectedness that gives particular ideas a compelling quality of importance.[1] In the following examination of traditional christology, I will focus on what I believe are some of the underlying connections of christological concepts to the larger social and psychological structures of the patriarchal family, especially its power orientations and its damage to self. I believe the patriarchal grounding of many classical christological ideas gives believers a feeling of the vast importance and sense of internal coherence of those ideas. In their time and context, the ideas may have had a transforming impact, but they do little now to demystify patriarchy or redeem humanity in its fullness.

I believe the images of the patriarchal family embedded in Christian theology are part of the emotional appeal of certain doctrines and of theology's patriarchal assumptions. As feminist theology seeks to draw us toward a nonpatriarchal future, analysis of the social, political, and psychological roots of doctrinal claims is crucial to demystifying nonliberating theological concepts and modern defenses of those concepts. The patriarchal underpinnings of many theological doctrines are, of course, not especially covert. The patriarchal structures manifest themselves especially clearly in the family analogies used to explain doctrinal statements.

The compelling power of many ideas lies in the images associated with them and in their unconscious association with unexamined but emotionally powerful experiences. The philosophical systems used to explain images often hide or flatten their psychological ability to invoke interest. The power of images is prior to and larger than their intellectual explanations, just as the intellectual development of a child is contingent upon the concrete world of objects it internalizes as resources for its self development. While theology cannot be reduced to sociology or psychology, new feminist insights in these areas need to inform our examination of the ultimate claims made by Christian theology so that we can develop more liberating theologies.

Beyond Jesus as the Christ

In moving beyond a unilateral understanding of power, I will be developing a christology not centered in Jesus, but in relationship and community as the whole-making, healing center of Christianity. In that sense, Christ is what I am calling Christa/Community.[2] Jesus participates centrally in this Christa/Community, but he neither brings erotic power into being nor controls it. He is brought into being through it and participates in the cocreation of it. Christa/Community is a lived reality expressed in relational images. Hence Christa/Community is described in the images of events in which erotic power is made manifest. The reality of erotic power within connectedness means it cannot be located in a single individual. Hence what is truly christological, that is, truly revealing of divine incarnation and salvific power in human life, must reside in connectedness and not in single individuals. The relational nature of erotic power is as true during Jesus' life as it is after his death. He neither reveals it nor embodies it, but he participates in its revelation and embodiment. And through its myriad embodiments and playful manifestations, we are led to take heart.

Heart—the self in original grace—is our guide into the territories of erotic power. Through that power we come to touch and be touched by, to transform and be transformed by all that is "the whole and compassionate being." But to come to that wisdom involves understanding the depth of the broken heart of patriarchy and its symbols. Christ, as the center of Christianity, will share in the patriarchal broken heart as long as it supports unilateral views of power. Feminism and Christianity can converge in love and justice if Christ can come to reveal erotic power. This feminist Christology, in being guided by heart, develops another way to understand Christ that will lead us away from the territories of patriarchy and into a world in which incarnation will refer to the whole of human life.

If Christa/Community can be presented as images of erotic power, divine power cannot be described in images of the patriarchal family, which crush heart, nor in the life of one heroic historical person who is singly identified as Christ. I will explore images that open us to the whole and compassionate being of divine incarnation and that illuminate the presence and work of erotic power, even in the brokenheartedness and crushed selves of the patriarchal family structures of Christianity. Erotic power exists as the vast process of human life itself, constantly flowing and growing in relationships; as the heart of Christianity, so, too, does Christ as Christa/Community.

The Abuse of the Son of God

While I do not advocate the continued exclusive or primary use of the image of God/dess as father, it has been a powerful and complex metaphor. The image contains nostalgic longing. A nurturing, intimate father is made virtually absent in patriarchal society. Yet persons need such love. A punitive or distant father in the face of such needs, combined with the inability of mothers to meet all the needs of a child and the tendency of mothers to use children for adult needs, can produce identification with the powerful father as a move toward self-protection. This process leaves the needs of children unmet. In a patriarchal culture, the theology of an abused child who needs love would, I think, be couched in terms of blame, guilt, and freedom from punishment through love from the parent perceived as most powerful. The damaged and defensive psyche requires the projection of the self's ambivalence onto an outside force or group and the rejection of those who might call such a system into question. This projection manifests itself strongly in Christianity in its hunt for and destruction of heretics and in its condemnation of pagans.

Alternatively, the longing for an intimate relationship with the father might be articulated in the image of a perfectly loving divine father who is not at all punitive and loves all creation unconditionally. But that father's affection, because it is largely unreal, would be distant, abstract, and impersonal. Such lack of real affection can be seen in doctrines of divine *apatheia* and in the assertion that the highest love is agape, a love based in objective dispassion.

In addition to the longing for a nonthreatening image of protection present in God/dess as father, the image can, in its best forms, produce a kind of community solidarity. The parental image can compel unity and tribal ethical obligation within a believing community, a concept of community which, in some more liberal theologies, is extended to all creation. Hence God/dess as father in liberal theology may have had the transforming impact of a metaphor that helps believers see their relationships in a new light. If one understands all other human beings as children of one father, one can assert that humanity is united as a family, even when reality contradicts such an assertion. However, the image seldom functions thus for women. It has led to the claim that all men are brothers under one father, leaving women outside the ecumenical brotherhood. In addition, the image of relationship via a parent places an intermediary as an outside authority that compels love by command.

Theological systems that carry a longing for an unreal past tend to prohibit our honest grounding in and real acceptance of our life experiences. Such systems of longing are based in nostalgia, the nostalgia of abused children, an abuse epidemic in patriarchal culture. Instead of grounding themselves in the experiences of touching heart to heart in erotic power and of profound love given us by others that we have internalized, such systems focus love on outside authority and obedience to another's will for us. Through being subject to unilateral power, we are supposed to realize mutuality and interdependence. In seeking to orient us to a transcendent, external power, such systems encourage faintheartedness and make self-awareness and personal power difficult. They foster dependence upon paternalism and engender the idea that divine power is unilateral. Those who seek to be honest about their experiences in patriarchal society will be most alienated from and most likely to reject the destructive and nostalgic elements of such theological systems. If we pay attention to the nostalgia, however, and read it for clues, rather than reject it outright, we can see what is missing here, which is interdependence—the intimacy, respect, and love necessary to loving the whole and compassionate being that comes from connectedness.

In theological analogies of father-son relationships, the parent and child are so fused that the parent is immersed in the child who, ideally, has no independent will. This parent-child fusion serves to maintain the independence of the parent and the dependence of the child. Classical trinitarian theology follows this model of paternalism. The father is independent of creation and the son issues from and is dependent on the father, even as the son coexists with the father at the beginning of creation. The aspect which coexists with the father, the logos, is that nature most fused with the father. Causality through divine will flows unilaterally from the father through his word to the son.

The fusion of parent and child is not the same as the empathy one person experiences when another suffers. Empathetic attunement prevents one person from inflicting suffering on another because the dignity and value of the other as a unique and distinct self is affirmed. Our ability to suffer with another empowers us, where possible, to stop suffering. The function of empathy is to prevent or stop suffering and self-sacrifice, not to inflict or to allow it.

The patriarchal father-god fosters dependence and, in his latent, punitive aspects, haunts many atonement doctrines. New Testament atonement images generally fall into four categories, according to J. F. Bethune-Baker in *An Introduction to the Early History of Christian Doctrine*: (1) through Jesus' death the enemies of God are reconciled to each other; (2) humanity is under bondage to sin, requiring Jesus' death as ransom; (3) sin causes humanity to be at a deficit so Jesus' death pays the debt; or (4) Jesus Christ is a propitiation, a pure sacrifice, who cleanses humanity of sin.[3] Trinitarian formulations connected to atonement stress the sacrifice of the father-god in taking on mortal life, so that he also suffers through the crucifixion. (This formula sounds like a variation of what parents say to children they punish, "This hurts me more than it hurts you.") The above understandings, begun "from above," from the divine aspect of Jesus as Christ, accept the need to protect authority.

Atonement christologies contain some notion of original sin, in which humanity is believed to be born with a tragic flaw. Therefore we must be dependent upon the perfect father to show us the way to a restored relationship with him and each other. The punishment of one perfect child has to occur before the father can forgive the rest of his children and love them. In more benign atonement forms, the father does not punish the son. Instead the father allows the son to suffer the consequences of the evil created by his wayward creation. Hence the father stands by in passive anguish as his most beloved son is killed, because the father refuses to interfere with human freedom. The sacrifice of this perfect son is the way to new life with the father for all those, who in their freedom, choose to believe someone else's suffering can atone for our flawed nature. The death and resurrection of this child are celebrated as salvific.

Trinitarian formulations of atonement absolve god the father of his punitive aspect by asserting that the consequences for human sin are actually taken into the divine existence, such that divine suffering takes away human suffering. This removal of suffering through the son's work reveals the truly loving divine nature. The human person who suffers the penalty for sin in this cosmic transaction is the one least deserving of punishment because he is the sinless son. In sacrificing his most beloved and only son, god the father demonstrates his love for all others. In believing that this transaction reveals the loving grace of god the father, the faithful are absolved of the need to suffer the consequences of sin. Rather than being cocreators and corevealers of grace, human beings are the dependent recipients of the fruits of an event working within a transcendent god. We are encouraged to believe our own suffering has been taken away by someone else's suffering and by a cosmic transaction within the divine life. If we are willing to remain dependent upon this power, we live in grace. The refusal to live in such dependence is sin, hubris, miring us in the consequences of a false sense of independence. What is missing in this scheme is interdependence and mutuality. We are not called to embrace our own suffering, to touch the deepest pain we feel about not having been loved and respected, and to discover the gifts of grace in our connectedness to ourselves and others. Instead we are enjoined to look to a suffering and power outside us, both greater than ours.

The shadow of omnipotence haunts atonement. The ghost of the punitive father lurks in the corners. He never disappears even as he is transformed into an image of forgiving grace. Hence the experience of grace is lodged, I believe, not so much in a clear sense of personal worth gained from an awareness of interdependence and the unconditional nature of love, but in a sense of relief from escaping punishment for one's failings. Paternalistic grace functions by allowing a select group to be in a favored relationship with the powerful father, but the overall destructiveness of the oppressive systems of the patriarchal family is not challenged by such benevolence. Hence judgment on the unsaved is a necessary component of atonement.

Such doctrines of salvation reflect by analogy, I believe, images of the neglect of children or, even worse, child abuse, making it acceptable as divine behavior—cosmic child abuse, as it were. The father allows, or even inflicts, the death of his only perfect son. The emphasis is on the goodness and power of the father and the unworthiness and powerlessness of his children, so that the father's punishment is just, and children are to blame. While atonement doctrines emphasize the father's grace and forgiveness, making it seem as if he accepts all persons whole without the demand that they be good and free of sin, such acceptance is contingent upon the suffering of the one perfect child.

The tendency to accept blame for being wrong is characteristic of an abused child, as Miller points out. The child projects the image of an ideal parent onto an outside figure who is always right and who is the source of both love and righteous punishment. Such projection helps the child manage a sense of rage about being denied love, being hurt, and being made wrong.

In addition, the child comes to associate hurt with love. Such an association also leads to a need to avoid the hurt by splitting off frightening or negative aspects from the self and projecting them onto others, as Christian theology has tended to do to women, pagans, Jews, and all "unsaved" others who are ready scapegoats.

Classical trinitarian formulas reflect patriarchal family relationships between parent and child and husband and wife. In the patriarchal family, all members are regarded as possessions and extensions of the reigning authority figure. The father and son become one person. The father is seen to live some aspect of his own life in his son. This fusion is repeated in the bridegroom-bride images of Jesus Christ and church. Hence humanity is fused to the son through our common human nature and to the son and the father through the spirit. The very abstractness and incoherence of the doctrines, with the continual need in the tradition for reexplanation and rationalization, indicate to me that they tend to reinforce mystifying images and a sense of fusion, which is part of human experience. But fusion cannot satisfy our deepest spiritual needs for images of intimacy. Real intimacy is grounded in the contextual, unique, and particular, and in interdependence.

Believing that we have already been forgiven for our sin by a previous act of divine grace through the suffering of the son can lead to self-acceptance and forgiveness of others. Being liberated from the fear of punishment produces an open graciousness toward others as happened in Luther's awakening to grace. However, traditional doctrinal formulations do nothing to transform dualistic and punitive patriarchal family structures, as can be seen in Luther's virulent anti-Semitism. Traditional theologies remain focused on the dependent relation of individual believers to a transcendent father. There is little in traditional doctrines to lead us to a concrete analysis of the social dimensions of sin or to a social sense of incarnation. We fail to see the suffering that is built into the social structures in which we all participate and our responsibility for the transformation of such structures, a critique of individualism in Christianity well articulated in liberation theologies.

Other nontrinitarian christological positions, those often labeled heretical such as Arianism, are not free from the tendency to move toward a fusion, though Arius held more of a distinction between father and son, such that the son only knew, in a creaturely way, what the father let him know. Nonetheless, the son lives his life in the father. Nontrinitarian formulas such as Apollinarianism or monotheletism carry the fusion to extremes and remove the crucial element of the fusion of Jesus with humanity by removing him too far toward the divine.[4]

The Modern Liberation of Jesus

The term "historical Jesus" identifies the Jesus of the Gospels and what can be known historically about him through biblical scholarship. The quest of the historical Jesus, in both the nineteenth and twentieth centuries, is extremely important in modern christologies. The quest emphasizes the humanity of Jesus in an unprecedented way and challenges christologies that proclaimed Jesus as the agent of universal divine action through rejection of his physical existence. His historical life and actual world have become important. In addition, research on the historical Jesus has provided invaluable information about the origins of Christianity. It is no longer possible to write about Jesus without mentioning his humanity and the eschatological character of his message. The quest has also helped make clear the limits of what can be known about Jesus as a historical person.

Modern incarnational christologies emphasize the life of the historical Jesus as revelatory of divine will. Liberation ideas stress his work for the poor and dispossessed and his vision of the *basileia*, the community of divine presence. Jesus is depicted as a heroic savior figure who defies established authority and reveals, through his work and the events of his life, the liberating will of the deity he worships. Hence he is actualizing his father's will. Modern atonement doctrines proclaim the life and death of Jesus as uniquely revealing our knowledge of God/dess. They emphasize what was accomplished in Jesus Christ for all human beings. Jesus becomes the spiritual heroic warrior, the single conqueror who defeats death, injustice, or evil. Most liberation christologies base themselves in some version of the sin/salvation paradigm of atonement, although the definition of sin has moved beyond individual blame to a more Marxist-based social understanding of sin. Liberation christologies emphasize Jesus' heroic aspect and obedience to his father. In addition, they affirm Jesus as the human vehicle of a saving and liberating knowledge of God/dess.

Feminist christologies, in various forms, also focus on Jesus as Christ, though they are careful not to make Jesus an exclusive revelation of God/dess. Patricia Wilson-Kastner equates feminist wholeness with the christological theme of reconciliation. She translates wholeness into an inclusive model of humanity and asserts that in the specific human being, Jesus, divine love was revealed.

> Jesus became flesh so as to show forth the love of God among us, a love which is not merely an expression of good will, but the power of an

energy which is the heart, core, and cohesive force of the universe.
[p. 90]

Wilson-Kastner acknowledges that an exalted view of Jesus' maleness has led
to rampant misogyny in the church and criticizes attempts to absolutize any
particular concrete aspect of an individual's personality. In developing an
inclusive christology she asserts that Christ as Jesus reveals the nature of love
as it continues to exist into the present.

> Christ is the human expression of God to us, and thus we must try to
> understand what God meant in Christ. . . . Christ is not simply the
> new male person, but one who shows all persons how to live. As a human
> he shows us what human self-possession and self-giving are. Thereby
> Christ shows us the link between divine and human, the cosmos and its
> conscious inhabitants. . . . The Christ whom we are considering is,
> after all, the living Christ, not simply a Palestinian rabbi of the first
> century. [p. 91]

On the one hand, Wilson-Kastner claims that Jesus is *a* human who reveals
divine love. On the other, she asserts that, at his crucifixion, he becomes *the*
new human being, the perfect priest who, as Christ, gathers into himself all
alienating dualisms that fragment the human condition. In this shift of
meaning, Wilson-Kastner retreats from an earlier assertion that the full
inclusion of the concrete particulars of any individual life or of any distinctive group of people is essential to understanding wholeness and developing
an adequate theology. An adequate theology must include those particulars
by basing itself in the whole human community.

> To gain new insights today, one needs to take into account a variety of
> perspectives, and find a firmer, more plausible base for theology. That
> base must involve both the whole human community, not just a part of
> that community, and the God who is the source of the whole. . . . If our
> fundamental relationship lies in human unity, then *all* values and deci-
> sions which are made by humans must take account of the whole. Such
> decision-making involves not only a balancing and weighing of many
> factors respecting individual diversity but also the complexity of our
> interrelationships. [p. 65]

I believe Wilson-Kastner retreats from the full implications of her position
when she begins to talk about Christ. Her retreat involves several shifts.

First, she takes what I have identified as the feminist sense of the whole and compassionate being—the necessity of our connection to the largest possible actual existence and the profound positive affirmation of the diversity of life—and shifts to the more monolithic and abstract Christian concept of unity that makes concrete particularity secondary. In doing so, she claims one human person embodies unity, rather than the whole set of interconnections in any person's community. This shift involves, I think, Wilson-Kastner's implicit assumption that human differences, which emerge from the reality of our concrete particularity, are the causes of alienation and destruction in human relationships. Her solution to this tendency toward alienation is unity. The positive reality of every person's distinctive differences from others, the ebb and flow of relationships, and our profound cocreation of each other is subsumed under the negative aspects of differences. She then asserts the human race as a unifying principle. Consequently, one person can fuse the complexity of the human condition into his one being as a representative of the human race.

In assuming the divisive nature of particularity, she asserts that the concrete particulars of Jesus' life are examples of God/dess's humility and self-emptying. She makes the actuality of Jesus, as an embodied human person, secondary to the universal, abstract principle of overcoming dualism. On the one hand, she states that the crucified Christ does not catch all up into an undifferentiated whole in which multiplicity is erased. On the other, she says:

> Because of the unity of divinity and humanity in the crucified Christ, the God who is self-giving and receiving accepts the fragmented human condition into the divine life for healing, and the humanity of Christ gathers into himself all the forces of alienation and destruction active in his own death. All the dualisms which divide, separate, cause pain, and support oppression and lack of communion with the others are all gathered together at the crucifixion, and Christ receives them. . . . Everything converges in him, and in his person and activity everything finds wholeness and meaning. [p. 100]

Thus Jesus becomes an exception to the concrete nature of human beings, rather than an example of it. No single human person except Jesus represents wholeness. For after his death, Wilson-Kastner claims, the entire church becomes the Christ.

Another shift occurs when Wilson-Kastner expands logos to include Wisdom, which, for her, makes the incarnation both masculine and feminine and affirms interdependence. She also intends with this shift to affirm the infinite variety of concrete interrelationships and shifting activities. This inclusion of feminine and masculine in the divine incarnation moves her toward an androgynous christology, which is consistent with her need to make Jesus as inclusive an image as possible.

Rosemary Ruether points out in *To Change the World* that androgynous christologies are not inclusive, even while claiming that Jesus as the Christ represents an inclusive concept of humanity. The symbol of Jesus is not fully egalitarian because no woman is allowed to represent full human potential.

> The very concept of androgyny presupposes a psychic dualism that iden-tifies maleness with one-half of human capacities and femaleness with the other. . . . Men gain their "feminine" side, but women contribute to the whole by specializing in the representation of the "feminine," which means exclusion from the exercise of the roles of power and leadership associated with masculinity. [pp. 49–53]

In any case, androgyny is not as egalitarian as it sounds. The male Yahweh has a long history of androgynous qualities, as king, father, and lover, with both controlling and loving characteristics. In a patriarchal social structure women are understood to be extensions of the male self and his needs, such that the nurturing, loving aspects of femininity can be sub-sumed under and within the masculine self. That Yahweh as father can have feminine qualities does not challenge or even demystify patriarchal struc-tures. An androgynous Jesus Christ also repeats a patriarchal pattern. Wis-dom, or Sophia, is not currently a feminine equivalent to Yahweh or logos, though we might work to make her so.

It may seem a solution to the church's tendency to deify Jesus' maleness to make human concreteness secondary to an abstract notion of his human-ness, which symbolizes unity. But such a view of unity produces another problem. Wilson-Kastner asserts that Jesus' revelation of divine love and his death reveal unity. If one individual comes to reveal unity, then I believe the concept of unity becomes detached from unity as interconnectedness, which can only be embodied in its fullness in the actuality of relationships.

At this point, I think Wilson-Kastner is using two notions of unity as one. The struggle that each of us encounters to make a coherent unity or whole of our lives, through all the complex relational elements that are our identity, is always limited and culturally bound, no matter how inclusive our actual world. That achievement of integrity, that depth of heart, is distinct, though not opposite, from the achievement of community, in which everyone must be present for unity to exist. In fact, I would argue that the second kind of unity is prior to and crucial to the formation of the first. Our real experiences of each other are crucial to our understanding of existence and of God/dess, as well as to a wholeness that moves toward the acceptance of cultural relativity and a capacity to connect to all that exists. Wilson-Kastner makes the first kind of unity prior to the second.

She also confuses wholeness with the first kind of unity by uncritically mixing concrete feminist political analyses of oppression and liberation with the more abstract philosophical notions of unity and reconciliation drawn from Christian theology. When feminists use the term wholeness, it carries concrete physical, psychological, political, economic, and sociological connotations. When Christians speak of unity, they are usually referring to doctrinal unanimity, which carries philosophical connotations. Wilson-Kastner jumps from one to the other without demonstrating how they are similar. In doing so, I think she attenuates the importance of real experience and concrete reality in feminist thought, thereby confusing unity with connectedness.

Wilson-Kastner deems inessential the very ways human beings are in the world. Concrete particulars are the evidence and channels of erotic power. The gift of the world to us and God/dess in the world come to us *through* embodiment. We do not experience ourselves or other persons as abstract principles or as general human beings, but as concretely present—as black tall man, Latin old woman, Korean small newborn, blond fat man, and so on. We come to love each other not through abstractions, but through the complex, ambiguous realities of our own unique existences. Our abstractions emerge from the concrete, fluid realities of our rich inner object world. Our ideas and images well up from there. That inner world is a mirror of the concrete outer world, even as it creatively appropriates that world.

The use of a notion like "the human race" as the key to understanding Jesus' significance sustains an inadequate feminist understanding of wholeness. To say that concrete particulars are examples of God/dess's humility in incarnation reduces to secondary status all the rich, complex, relational elements that make us human persons. Concreteness is taken as incidental to or transcended by Jesus' incarnation of the divine Logos. Yet Jesus' world and divine power in that world are incarnate in him in the distinctive complexity of his own life. And that life was as limited and culturally bound as any human life. The concreteness of our own lives comes from interconnection in particular contexts and reveals erotic power. Hence others are essential for wholeness to occur. Wholeness as community cannot be summed up in one life.

We are uniquely constituted by a complexity of characteristics that are the fullness of our being. The whole-hearted inclusion of the concrete particulars of life affirms the interactions of erotic power in the world. The fullness of humanity is the presence of erotic power in each individual-in-community and in the constant change and growth of each moment of existence. We continue to become the fullest incarnation of erotic power when our bodies, feelings, needs, and awarenesses are affirmed as an integral aspect of our ongoing existence and as the route of our connection to and cocreation of others. Christian idealism and its dualistic mind-body split has consistently subordinated the physical, or matter and earth, to the spiritual, or soul and heaven.

When in our definition of human perfection we make evidence of erotic power secondary to the soul or spirit, the complex elements that uniquely constitute each of us are subordinated to our abstract inclusion in Jesus as the Christ. That which we have denied as central to another becomes difficult to affirm within ourselves. Affirming Jesus' particularity in its diverse forms as an aspect of God/dess and the world in him allows us to acknowledge how he differs from us and to affirm that we ourselves and our world incarnate God/dess. Hence particularity is not the self-emptying of divine power, but an aspect of its fullness. Jesus was cocreated by his world, as we are by ours.

Rosemary Ruether, in constructing her position on christology, criticizes androgynous christologies (discussed above) and spirit christologies. Spirit christologies disembody the spiritual dimension from the concrete, historical Jesus, calling the former aspect Christ. Through such spiritualizing of Christ, various groups, such as the Shakers, have claimed a reincarnation of Christ in new form. Though such spirit christologies allow for the claim that Christ can take female form, they do so at the expense of the body. According to Ruether, nothing in spirit christologies allows us the positive reclamation of female bodies or profound relationships to nature. I believe she is on the right track in refuting attempts to spiritualize Christ. The disembodiment of Christ from Jesus and reembodiment of Christ in a new single savior allows the claim that one human form, male or female, is Christ, locating power unilaterally in one place. However, I believe Ruether's own position raises other difficulties because she operates partially from an underlying unilateral view of power.

Jesus' criticisms of religious and social hierarchy, according to Ruether, parallel feminist criticisms of patriarchy. She uses the model of the prophetic tradition to demonstrate the validity of his redemptive role in human life. As prophet, Jesus proclaims a new vision of relationship to God/dess and the world, a vision that is nonhierarchical and iconoclastic.

> Jesus as liberator calls for a renunciation, a dissolution, of the web of status relationships by which societies have defined privilege and deprivation. He protests against the identification of this system with the favor or disfavor of God. His ability to speak as liberator does not reside in his maleness but in the fact that he has renounced this system of domination and seeks to embody in his person the new humanity of service and mutual empowerment. He speaks to and is responded to by low-caste women because they represent the bottom of this status network and have the least stake in its perpetuation. [1983, p. 137]

Jesus reveals a new divine call to liberation that transcends all status and privilege. The prophetic behavior of Jesus is evidence for the compatibility of feminism with Christianity. Ruether believes Jesus' maleness reveals the

> *kenosis of patriarchy*, the announcement of the new humanity through a lifestyle that discards hierarchical caste privilege and speaks on behalf of the lowly. [1983, p. 137]

Jesus is the one who morally transcends patriarchy. Hence Jesus is the authority and evidence of feminist Christianity.

The historical Jesus starts a process. Ruether, like Wilson-Kastner, does not want to limit Christ to Jesus. She urges that the relationship between redeemer and redeemed be seen as a fluid interaction, so that the redeemer is one who has been redeemed. "Those who have been liberated can, in turn, become paradigmatic, liberating persons for others" (1984, p. 138). Reuther disavows the "once-for-all" redemption of Jesus and speaks of Christic personhood continuing in all liberated humanity.

> Christ, the liberated humanity, is not confined to a static perfection of one person two thousand years ago. Rather, redemptive humanity goes ahead of us, calling us to yet incompleted dimensions of human liberation. [1983, p. 138]

While Jesus is the first prophetic Christ, the coming reign of God/dess will be the second coming.

The difficulty I find with Ruether's position is her move from a nonrelational paradigm to a relational one. The biblical prophet is the heroic individual, someone who receives a private revelation of God/dess and then proclaims it against all odds. The prophet, isolated and persecuted, preaches a message about proper worship of the one true God/dess. Few prophetic images connote receptivity toward, listening to, or interaction with a community of support. The prophet seeks to protect the sovereignty of divine will against any who threaten it.

In placing Jesus' fullest relationship to God/dess within a prophetic context, the world to which Jesus subsequently preaches and ministers becomes the objective proof of his private relationship with God/dess. For the prophet characteristically has a private experience of God/dess and obeys by protecting divine rule. Jesus' iconoclastic and serving relationship to the world is evidence of his right to be called Christ. The world becomes the proving ground of his personal relationship to God/dess and of his unilateral power. As liberated man, he liberates and empowers others. The oppressed function, in Ruether's scheme, as victims to be acted upon. The world is not described as constitutive of Jesus' personal awareness of God/dess or as a source of his power. Jesus is the hero and liberator. While Ruether claims the redeemer is also redeemed, she gives no evidence for how, since only the liberated can liberate. The relationship of liberator to oppressed is unilateral. Hence the hero must speak *for* victims. The brokenhearted do not speak *to* the strong. I believe Ruether maintains a unilateral, heroic model.

The iconoclastic function of the Gospels has been much examined for its capacity to affirm justice and shatter patriarchy. The clean fury of prophetic iconoclasm is essential to the shattering of complacency and entrenched power structures. This shattering is crucial to the powers of the weak—to the capacity of those on the underside of hierarchies to be skeptical of dominant forms of thought and to think in new ways. At the political level, iconoclasm works to demystify the dominant power of the ruling elite. At the personal level, the orientation of the broken heart toward controlling power and defensive rigidity is challenged. However, the shattering is only half the story.

Ruether maintains a concrete and historical understanding of Jesus as Christ the liberator and does not want to limit Christ to Jesus. However, while Jesus is alive, he is the Christ. Jesus challenges social structures. Reuther's emphasis on the need to change social structures is essential to any feminist understanding of Christianity. Anger is an essential step toward liberation, but liberation is one element in relationships. Iconoclasm remains too polarizing to sustain.

The rebellion against paternalism and oppression is an important step of anger, but being stuck in anger can lead to a rigid self-righteousness that is not self-critical or to an unconscious reenactment of power over others. The shattering of dominant power must be accompanied by a move toward self-awareness and self-affirmation. The continual focus on political structures outside the self—on positional power—cuts us off from important and potentially liberating insights through the self. The skepticism that challenges hierarchy comes from a community that supports and empowers demystification. Missing from Ruether's position is the crucial presence of members of Jesus' community as embodying God/dess and having a transforming impact on him. Without alternative relationships, the iconoclastic shattering of power-over is also the fragmentation of self. We require relationships that support us to develop the play space that can see through destructive powers, even our own.

The Jesus of Erotic Power and the Feminist Christa/Community

The interactive process of erotic power makes essential the give and take quality of intimacy among selves. Decisions and actions are not made by one person, but result from historical circumstances and from our deep relatedness to other persons. I believe the above views of Christ tend to rely on unilateral views of power and a too limited understanding of the power of community. They present a heroic Jesus who alone is able to achieve an empowering self-consciousness through a solitary, private relationship with God/dess. If Jesus is reported to have been capable of profound love and concern for others, he was first loved and respected by the concrete persons of his life. If he was liberated, he was involved in a community of mutual liberation, which Ruether states but does not demonstrate in her model of Jesus. The Gospel narratives give us glimpses of the mutuality of Jesus' relationships in their pictures of Capernaum, a place to which Jesus repeatedly returns for support and nurturing, and in the settings of the stories in which Jesus is visiting the houses of his friends for conversation and physical comfort. Even during his most active ministry, he rarely goes anywhere alone; one of the first acts of that ministry was to call others to participate in creating the *basileia*, the community of God/dess.

Jesus' vision of *basileia* grew to include the dispossessed, women, and non-Jews, a group Schüssler Fiorenza calls "the marginal," because of his encounter and interaction with the real presence of such people. They cocreate liberation and healing from brokenheartedness. They reveal heart. Relationships create the possibility of a new vision, for in the power of real presence, erotic power—divine incarnate power—works. Direct, firsthand, deeply felt contact produces shared understandings and transforming insights. The visions that empower the actions of a community are not possible before the actual relationships. The feminist term "woman-identified" means the capacity to feel and envision justice for women on the basis of concrete relationships with real women, rather than on the predefined concepts of androcentric world views.

If feminism can be reconciled with Christianity, such reconciliation is not possible because Jesus, as the heroic figure, reveals a nonpatriarchal vision of community in which women may participate. The reconciliation is possible because of the work of women and because feminist insights about erotic power intersect with the Christian confession that divine reality and redemptive power are love in its fullness. Using feminist experiences and analyses of male dominance and a feminist hermeneutic of erotic power on the biblical texts, it is possible to catch glimpses, within androcentric texts, of the important presence and influence of erotic power within the Christa/ Community. Erotic power in the texts sustains and cocreates the whole and compassionate being.

This feminist reformulation of christology depends upon the works of those feminists cited above. My position moves in a different direction in feminist territories, but it could not have been developed without the dislocation from androcentric realms that feminist theology has encouraged. I believe that feminist theological visions of new territories are well on their way to charting a clearer, truer route to justice, love, and peace. I will explore christology constructed on the assumption that divine erotic power liberates, heals, and makes whole through our willingness to participate in mutuality. What follows is a christology of interconnection and action for justice, love, and peace, not of authority, heroism, and proclamation. I find glimpses of this christology of erotic power in the Markan miracle stories, in exorcism and the healing of brokenheartedness—in the Christa/Community of erotic power. I also find it in the Markan passion narrative as the community confronts one of the most serious threats to its existence.

The Redemption of Christa/Community

Christa/Community emerges from, reveals, and recreates erotic power as it moves to include the whole and compassionate being. Even in Jesus' lifetime, Christa/Community is not simply the figure of Jesus combined with an abstract ideal, but the members of his whole community who generate erotic power. Christa/Community involves his community's experience of him, but Christa/Community is not limited to the historical Jesus, even in his lifetime.

To base a christology largely on the historical Jesus, as Schubert Ogden in *The Point of Christology* claims, is to commit the "fallacy of misplaced concreteness," a term coined by Whitehead in *Science and the Modern World*.[5] We confuse some concept with the larger context and events from which it is drawn, mistaking the concept for the entire phenomenon. This fallacy dooms a civilization to sterility when its abstractions cannot burst through to the larger context of reality from which abstractions are taken. Tom Driver in *Christ in a Changing World* argues on ethical grounds that Christ understood as Jesus must be removed as the center of Christianity because keeping Jesus Christ in the center gives priority to individual existence instead of the larger sanctity of community.[6] For Driver, even when Christ is decentralized, Christ refers to individuals within specific communities, to many Christs. I believe the individualizing of Christ misplaces the locus of incarnation and redemption. We must find the revelatory and saving events of Christianity in a larger reality than Jesus and his relationship to God/dess or any subsequent individual Christ.

Both the old and new quests of the historical Jesus presuppose the primary importance of the individual. However, individuals only make sense in the larger context of events embedded in particular historical structures. The tendency to focus on heroes may divert our attention from the factors most important in understanding an event. Events emerge from enormous social-cultural factors as well as from unique individuals who participate in the making of events. Elisabeth Schüssler Fiorenza's *In Memory of Her* illustrates the shift in perspective that can grow from a look at larger historical and cultural factors in the formation of Christianity. The historical information gained by feminist biblical scholars is crucial to a new understanding of the origins of Christianity.

This new understanding does not come simply from better history. Many feminist theologians are also calling for a change in standards of truth and authority. The shift in standards to women's experiences under patriarchy and the call for liberating theories and action is creating a new vision of Christian faith. In *House for Hope: a Study in Process and Biblical Thought* William Beardslee states:

> One who proclaims the Christian faith is a poet, creating a convincing world of vision with the figure of Christ at its center...the poet is actually creating a world in which the response can be meaningful; he calls for a shift or change in...standards.[7]

The feminist shift in standards creates new visions that are moving toward a different center for Christian faith.

The shift in perspective suggested here relocates Christ in the community of which Jesus is one historical part. Jesus is used by the Gospel writers, who shape oral and written traditions for their own distinctive theological purposes, to focus faith, but he is not the locus of the redemptive event, even during his life. Christ—the revelatory and redemptive witness of God/dess's work in history—is Christa/Community. The Christa/Community in the biblical texts, in the stories of Jesus and other figures, is the church's imaginative witness to its experiences of brokenness and sacredness of erotic power in human existence.

The Gospel writers use Jesus, his community, a past faith heritage, and their own life contexts to create distinctive images of faith and hope. Some of the images support male dominance and unilateral power, reinforcing brokenheartedness; others do not. Images such as king, lord, shepherd, and warrior used to describe Jesus' power focus on dominance, images not surprising in a patriarchal tradition. Although power as dominance relies on a relational matrix for its existence, it weakens, rather than strengthens, that matrix and creates brokenheartedness. The life-giving tension in the biblical texts is the continual movement away from patriarchal values, even within images of patriarchy.

Images of dominance are often linked to images such as servant that undercut dominance, reflecting an ambivalence about hierarchical powers. Few of the Gospel accounts of the followers of Jesus indicate anyone high up in hierarchical structures. The formation of the early community involved the powers of the weak—a skepticism about the ideology of ruling hierarchies of power and the creation of support communities oriented around action for the weak. All of the sayings about the coming *basileia* announce the defeat of oppressive powers. The miracle stories proclaim the defeat even more vehemently through the activity of the community and demonstrate the healing power of the human heart.

Many of the images used in the past to speak of the relationships within the Christian community focus on Jesus' self-sacrificial death and on the true nature of the highest form of love as agape, as selfless giving, reflecting a healthy skepticism about the destructiveness of egocentric greed and power. But the opposite pole of egocentricity, egoless self-sacrifice, does not lead to love or intimacy, for love and intimacy require self-awareness, self-affirmation, and concrete presence. Erotic power and heart are the basis of love. Once the open, interactive spaces of erotic power and heartfelt relationships in society are opened, what kind of christology will lead us to the territories of erotic power?

The Christa/Community of erotic power is the connectedness among the members of the community who live with heart. Christa/Community evidences heart, which is the conduit in human existence of erotic power. The hermeneutic tool that guides the following investigation of the miracle and passion stories in the Gospel of Mark is the search for Christa/Community in images of heart.

·4·

The Gospel of Mark:
Erotic Power at Work

T his journey into the territories of erotic power is easily seen in several Markan examples of exorcism and healing. The stories symbolize the political, social, psychological, and relational nature of sickness, the necessity for heart, and the interactions of erotic power. They are stories of the dynamics of heart.

Mark is important in the study of the synoptic Gospels as an early attempt to shift from Christian reliance on oral transmission to literary tradition. Biblical scholars have demonstrated its importance as an influence on Matthew and Luke. The Markan omission of all but the bare bones of the Christa/Community's activity during Jesus' lifetime, the lack of aggrandizing, sermonic material about Jesus, and the focus on action give a sharp, event-oriented quality to the Gospel. The Gospel's primary concern seems less with Jesus' sayings and more with what happened within and to the community that included Jesus. In addition, as I will argue in chapter 5, in the passion narrative the legendary, heroic Jesus shifts to a shadowy, desperate Jesus who becomes a catalyst of events rather than the center of the community, a shift that leaves an ambiguous, open-ended finish.

Elisabeth Schüssler Fiorenza believes Mark also is important as a Gospel that struggles to avoid patterns of dominance and submission. Those who are the farthest from power as dominance—slaves, children, and women—become the paradigms of true discipleship, and, I would add, the revealers of heart.

> Leaders and highly esteemed members of the community must become equal with the lowest and socially weakest members of the community by becoming their servants and slaves. . . . Whereas post-Pauline writers

71

advocate adaptation to their society in order to lessen tensions within that society and thus to minimize the suffering and persecution of Christians, the writer of Mark's Gospel insists on the necessity of suffering and makes it quite clear that such suffering must not be avoided, especially not by adapting the structures of Christian community and leadership to Greco-Roman structures of dominance and submission.[1]

The unilaterally powerful messianism early in Mark gives way, according to Elizabeth Struthers Malbon in *Narrative Space and Mythic Meaning in Mark*, to a suffering messianism as Jesus seeks to reveal the significance of suffering as opposed to power. Mark's focus on suffering is a revelation that challenges oppositions and mediates them into a mythic whole that is not a goal or a set of boundaries, but a way, a dynamic process of movement.

> Being on the way is not static but dynamic. . . . Life in Galilee, though filled with experiences of a new power, was not without its problems for Jesus and his followers. . . . Thus to be on the way to Galilee is not to escape the challenges of life but to risk involvement in the paradox of power and suffering. . . . The tension of the Markan ending reflects the tension of the Good News according to Mark: conflict between the chaos and order of life is overcome not in arriving, but in being on the way. [pp. 167–68]

Exorcism and Healing: The Work of Erotic Power

The miracle stories are the most neglected in christological discussions, except when they are discussed in conservative circles as evidence of Jesus' dominant power over destructive forces and proof of his divinity, or when they are given "natural" or allegorical explanations in liberal circles. The exorcisms and healings have not been understood as normative statements about the sacred within the Christian community. I will make them so in this study. If these stories are understood as paradigmatic statements of divine activity, other aspects of the community's witness can be understood within the root metaphors of exorcism and healing which convey the meaning of wholeness and of Christa/Community as a relational event.

If these stories are to be paradigmatic christological statements, they should not be understood as stories of the return of life to a status quo equilibrium. Nor should they be understood as an attempt to reassert an outmoded supernaturalism. In *The Oral and Written Gospel* Werner Kelber claims the primary function of exorcism and healing, unlike the parables, is to fight instability and restore the structures of the human lifeworld.[2] Hence they reconcile alienation in a culture-supportive manner. The stories use dramatic action to heighten the picture of Jesus' struggle with death-dealing powers and to produce a resolution that is in continuity with culture.

> Accommodation to the world is aspired. . . . Far from arousing questions about culture, they extend certainties and promise social stability. [p. 74]

Kelber's claims about the stabilizing function of exorcism and healing ignore the political dimensions of such acts. Kelber seems to assume that the project of making whole the lives of the oppressed does not subvert patriarchal culture. To the contrary, such a project undertaken within hierarchical structures challenges the status quo. Miracle-working charismatics like Jesus and the community of healers who worked with him did not commonly restore privileged classes to their positions.

In contrast to Kelber, Antoinette Clark Wire, in "The Structure of the Gospel Miracle Stories and Their Tellers," argues that the miracle stories and their arrangement intend to show the presence of an oppressive social context and the breaking of it.[3] Hence the world of the sufferer is a clue to what is overcome by healing. Schüssler Fiorenza contends that the miracle stories especially provide a clear vision of human life lived in divine power, a vision that is not possible with the maintenance of oppressive power structures.

> The *basileia* vision of Jesus makes people whole, healthy, cleansed, and strong. It restores people's humanity and life. The salvation of the *basileia* is not confined to the soul but spells wholeness for the total person in her/his social relations. [p. 123]

In *The Miracle Stories of the Early Christian Tradition* Gerd Theissen also claims that the miracle stories have a world-transforming function.[4] They restore to the hearer the importance of the "passionate subjectivity" that comes from the symbolic action of "an adult subject reaching back to his childhood" (p. 289). In reaching back, the negativity of existence can be transformed. The stories insist that the possessed be freed, the hungry fed, the sick cured, and the blind made to see. Images of wholeness for those who challenge existing power structures are pitted against the realisms of the status quo that press toward conformity. Hence the presence of the broken-hearted illuminates a new reality by crossing boundaries that challenge ordinary existence. Thus the miracles reveal the sacred.

> Where a protest against human suffering takes place through a revelation of the sacred, the elimination of that suffering is not just desirable; it is not less than an obligation. . . . This is the final implication of the miracle stories: they will rather deny the validity of all previous experiences than the right of human suffering to be eliminated. [p. 302]

The implications of liberating and making whole the oppressed are lost if one understands miracles as attempts to restore the status quo. The passionate subjectivity revealed through the biblical texts crosses boundaries and illuminates the sacred. Actions to heal brokenheartedness shatter old orientations to self and power and open fissures that birth erotic power.

In the twentieth century, returning to exorcism and healing can seem like a step backward into the dark ages of witch burning, magic, and belief in demons and angels. Emphasizing objectivity and the scientific method gives us a greater sense of control over human pain and suffering. Yet science has often been used to "prove" the racist, class, and sexist ideologies of Western culture. Also, the scientific method has tended to ignore subjective factors in understanding disease. And the mode of scientific inquiry fostered by Western thought has not tended to challenge the basic imperialistic, militaristic, dualistic values of our capitalist, patriarchal culture. As a tool, like religion, science has often served the reigning power structures.

The rational-scientific view of disease has its roots in Greek philosophy and represents the use of objective knowledge, rather than compassion or magic, to cure insanity and disease. By the Reformation period, healing had been deemed a dispensation for a former time, and Luther ruled that healing acts by contemporaries were works of the devil. The Enlightenment, with its trust in scientific reason and its devaluation of the supernatural, relegated exorcism and miraculous healing to the realms of superstition and belief in the supernatural. In a scientific age, miracles seem an embarrassment unless rational explanations can be made for them. Yet they constitute over a third of the Gospel narratives and figure prominently in Jesus' popularity and authority, and in his community's sense of the divine power at work in life.

Of course the rational-scientific view of disease has had important positive consequences. It allows for clear diagnoses of some diseases and the active use of a body of knowledge to treat emotional and physical pain. The focus on empirical, causal factors has resulted in the modern age either in the control or extinction of germ-related diseases such as smallpox, pneumonia, and syphilis, which once had serious consequences. We also a have somewhat more sophisticated understanding of human behavior through psychology and sociology.

The dualism that has pervaded modern science as a legacy of the Enlightenment, however, has also left us with new problems. Emotional and physical factors in illness are still largely divided into the separate, and often antagonistic, treatment spheres of medicine and psychology. In addition, the treatment of disease is focused, like Western religion, on the cure of the individual. While statistics are available on the impact of geography, economic and social status, race, religion, lifestyle, occupation, and gender on the nature and rate of disease, such factors are seldom treated as important factors in treating sickness. Hence the major institutions responsible for health in our society have tended to focus on the narrowest necessary causes of sickness, such as germs and genes, rather than on a unified field theory that understands sufficiently the causes of sickness to produce a healthy society. The three largest killers in First World countries, cancer, heart disease, and stroke, are too complex to be handled with current medical etiology. Finally, even diseases such as malnutrition that can be treated with individual cures are caused by human systems, as are diseases created by the use of science, diseases such as radiation poisoning, cancer, and chemical waste or pollution-related illnesses. These diseases are no less deadly than those caused by germs and genes, and they affect millions of the earth's peoples.

Our current age faces large-scale suffering delivered by the structures of our global political and economic systems, of which some of the most destructive are malnutrition, despair, depression, suicide, substance abuse, family violence, radiation poisoning, and the effects of terrorism, totalitarianism, and warfare. Our scientific age has brought us to the brink of a capacity to kill virtually all known life on our planet. The philosophical assumptions, research, and application methods of modern medicine have not been adequate to the task of producing healthy persons because they have been too locked into a dualistic, patriarchal world view to produce an inclusive, relational vision of wholeness.

The relegation of exorcism and healing to magic and superstition has cut us off from their transforming value. The feminist concern for psychic, spiritual, and physical healing and the feminist demystification of the medical establishment show the implications of a more holistic approach to sickness. I believe the biblical miracle stories may be more theologically significant than either conservatives or liberals have thought. The stories point to the political implications of disease and to the social-psychic nature of much sickness. They present inclusive and sophisticated metaphors for understanding the relational nature of sickness and suffering.

Sickness is oppression or possession by hostile forces that seek to destroy a person's body, psyche, spirit, and/or community. Sickness points to the social and relational dimensions of individual disease. Sickness reveals brokenheartedness and produces suffering. Brokenheartedness, as I use it, is a metaphor for both political oppression and sickness and the damage to the self from complex forms of destruction in our culture. In using the image of brokenheartedness I want to point to that which draws our attention to the large, relational dimensions of sickness that rest in economic, political, and environmental factors.

We are drawn to connect with others because their suffering compels us to understand. Brokenheartedness reveals our power to hurt each other and to heal each other. Hence brokenheartedness, when we can acknowledge it, reveals both the heart's original grace and its virtually indestructible presence. As events of connection—as stories that mediate opposites—the Markan miracle stories show a way to heal brokenheartedness and reveal erotic power in heart. Heart makes us pliant, flexible, tender, vulnerable—capable of being damaged. That damage comes as sickness, oppression, and self-hate. The healing possible through erotic power compels us to be more aware of heart and of the possibilities for living in grace. Heart thrives in the integrating play spaces of dream, myth, fantasy, and spirit, realms which include exorcism and healing.

The exorcisms and healings characterize the first part of Mark, chapters 1–10, the Galilean ministry. Chapter 10 links the first nine chapters, which emphasize the power of the *basileia*, with the Judean ministry of chapters 11–16, which focus on suffering, the topic of chapter 5 of this book.

Exorcising Demons: Liberating Work

The exorcism stories use demons to depict the loss of self-possession. They tell of persons possessed by destructive powers. In the first century such unfriendly forces were described in images of supernatural powers, but I do not believe the use of supernatural images makes these stories outmoded as theologically charged statements. The use of demons brings a religious dimension to political messages. But the exorcisms are not simply religious and other-worldly.

Images of exorcism can function as messages about political domination. Demon possession was a political reality in a time when loyalty to foreign rule carried the demand to worship foreign gods. Political oppression in its worst forms threatened the loss of personal integrity, the loss of internal subjectivity, and the repression of authentic relationships to self and others. Klaus Seybold and Ulrich B. Mueller argue in *Sickness and Healing* that the first-century political world and personal self-determination became parts of one cohesive reality.

> Foreign political domination was, for Jewish understanding, *eo ipso* associated with the concept of the reign of foreign gods or demons. . . . the external experience of powerlessness encountered in the face of this double oppression could be transferred to the interior.[5]

The Gospel images of demon possession are heavy with symbols of brokenheartedness and the absence of erotic power. The Gospels picture Roman oppression as demon possession. As Schüssler Fiorenza states:

> What we today call oppressive power structures and dehumanizing power systems, apocalyptic language calls "evil spirits," "Satan," "Beelzebub," demons. [p. 123]

The feminist concept of "the enemy within"—the internalization of a negative and destructive self-concept based on subordination by the dominant culture—and the Gospels' picture of exorcism intersect. The liberation of a person from internalized oppression signals the empowerment of the oppressed through self-possession, the potential defeat of political oppression, and the removal of power as control. In the biblical imagery of demons, blame for self-destructive behavior is removed from the sufferer to a source outside the afflicted. The presence of sickness itself, the possessed behavior, is the first clue that heart is at work within the possessed whose energies are fighting brokenheartedness. Therefore, instead of blaming the victim, we are compelled to feel solidarity with and compassion for the oppressed. The work of divine power through the exorcism of demons restores the person to heart—to relationships to self and other. Such exorcising work then indicates the presence of erotic power in the world, working within community and through each person to remove oppressive powers.

The story of the Gerasene Demoniac in Mark 5:1–20 is one obvious and vivid metaphor of internalized oppression. The Markan account tells of one so possessed that he suffered a living death. He lived among the tombs, and his self-destructiveness was mighty. He had wrenched apart the chains that bound him, and night and day among the tombs and on mountains he was always crying out, and cutting himself with stones.

> So they came to the other side of the lake, into the country of the Gerasenes. As he stepped ashore, a man possessed by an unclean spirit came up to him from among the tombs where he had his dwelling. He could no longer be controlled; even chains were useless; he had often been fettered and chained up, but he had snapped his chains and broken the fetters. No one was strong enough to master him. And so, unceasingly, night and day, he would cry aloud among the tombs and on the hill-sides and cut himself with stones. When he saw Jesus in the distance, he ran and flung himself down before him, shouting loudly, "What do you want with me, Jesus, son of the Most High God? In God's name do not torment me." (For Jesus was already saying to him, "Out, unclean spirit, come out of this man!") Jesus asked him, "What is your name?" "My name is Legion," he said, "there are so many of us." And he begged Jesus hard that Jesus would not send them out of the country. [*New English Bible*, Mark 5:1–10]

Here is a picture of a being so torn by internal conflicts, so damaged by forces outside himself, that he injured himself and lived among the dead—tombs—the most fearful realm of chaos, mentioned only again in reference to John (Mark 6:29) and Jesus (Mark 15:46). The demoniac lives where no one goes—a defiling, frightening place. But like Jesus later, he is about to leave.

Raging chaos, in the story just before (Mark 4:35–41), has been depicted as a storm-tossed sea. The demoniac's fury, like a stormy sea, sought to destroy the evidence of his loss of himself, his own body. But this injuring is itself the harbinger of redemption in the story, the first evidence of heart struggling to surface which initiates the field of erotic power. Someone is needed to calm the storm and the disciples, having crossed the sea with Jesus, know the power that stills the storm. A battle is raging between heart and Legion, but help has arrived.

Few first-century Jewish Christians would have missed the significance of Legion, the demons' name. Armies "there are so many of us," have invaded the demoniac and are on the defensive against Jesus who participates in a power greater than the destructive powers of political oppression. The demons possessing the demoniac, lacking courage, cry out against Jesus. In this story Jesus represents the emergence of a different power, the only power capable of restoring heart instead of imposing a new form of external control. Jesus reaches out with his own heart to touch the heart faintly glimmering under the cries of pain and shadows of death. The cries themselves are a demand for help, and life is restored in the work of erotic power. Calm returns. The man can leave his tombs.

To a first-century church living under the constant shadow of Roman persecution, the symbolism of death through loss of heart under political domination is powerful. The political reality imaged through demon possession removes any excuse for blaming the victim. Possession is not the result of personal sin and cannot be healed by private penance. The possession comes from relationships lived under the deceptions of unilateral power. A return to heart must come from the revelation of erotic power that emerges in the relationships possible through the exorcism.

> Now there happened to be a large herd of pigs feeding on the hill-side, and the spirits begged him, "Send us among the pigs and let us go into them." He gave them leave; and the unclean spirits came out and went into the pigs; and the herd, of about two thousand, rushed over the edge into the lake and were drowned. [*New English Bible*, Mark 5:11–13]

To further the irreverence toward the Roman occupation, playful ridicule is interjected. In trying to save themselves, the demons named Legion rush to invade pigs and are drowned in the sea. (This animal epithet symbolizing militaristic force returned as a lively metaphor in the American antiwar movement of the late 1960s.) The earlier chaotic sea returns for a sacred purpose. This reversal underscores the optimistic humor of the narrative in which the most profane of animals, symbol of political oppression, is drowned in chaos. The power to exorcise and heal includes and utilizes chaos and calms it when necessary.

Malbon has noticed interesting textual allusions in the use of the sea, described above, and in the use of mountains. The demoniac cries out from tombs and mountains. The swine are feeding near the mountain before the demons possess them. Like Isaac in the hands of Abraham, the demoniac is granted a pardon from death on the mountain by the presence of a substitutionary animal.

> Because of its nearness to heaven, the mountain serves as an archetypical
> location for divine rescue or healing and for the divine establishment of
> the community, old or new. [p. 85]

Possessed of his right mind and heart, the demoniac is urged to return to
his own people and to tell what divine power has done for him. The casting
out of Legion has required a power not contained in the conventional methods of oppressive power. The miraculous breaks in playfully via erotic power,
which, in structures of oppression, manifests itself in the courage to face
brokenheartedness, to cast out demons, and to touch heart to heart. When
the demoniac is tempted to give himself away in dependency by staying with
Jesus, he is told to return home and to tell the story of divine power.

In some of the exorcisms the demons struggle to maintain control far more
ferociously than Legion. In Mark 9:26 the demon convulses the person so
strongly that the boy is left in a coma as if dead. The young are especially
vulnerable. In that instance, driving the demon out is not enough, for the
sufferer has not enough heart to be separate from his own demons. Jesus
must take his hand. The touching of hands generates power. In this story as
in numerous others, an important aspect of the exorcisms is Jesus' acknowledgment of heart in the afflicted and his direct confrontation of the demons.
His action is usually swift and vehement and works much the way anger does
to separate the fusion of selves with powerful and overpowering others.

Exorcisms are often seen as heroic instances in which Jesus saves some
poor soul, thereby demonstrating his superior divine authority and combat-
ive power. Certainly the heightened sense of the miraculous and of Jesus'
superiority over other healers points to early Christian competitive interests
in the superiority of Christianity over all other cults of miracle charismatics.
But combined with the story of Jesus' temptation, the exorcisms lead to a
different interpretation that refutes a paternalistic interpretation: those who
have experienced oppression know how to touch hearts broken in similar
fashion. The exorcisms are not described as being conducted by someone
empowered by ruling authorities. The image of Jesus as exorcist is someone
who has experienced his own demons.

> Thereupon the Spirit sent him away into the wilderness, and there he re-
> mained for forty days tempted by Satan. He was among the wild beasts;
> and the angels waited on him. [New English Bible, Mark 1:12–13]

The temptation stories point to the image of a wounded healer, to an image
of one who by his own experience understands vulnerability and internalized

oppression. In having recovered their own hearts, healers have some understanding of the suffering of others.

Naming the demons means knowing the demons. If we have understood that naming the demons must come from the buried heart that yearns for erotic power, then helping another sufferer name demons is a reenactment of our own search for heart. We journey with another on a familiar road that leads into the territories of erotic power. The Gospels imply that anyone who exorcises cannot be a stranger to demons. Mark hints that Jesus has named his demons in his temptation in the wilderness, with the help of the angels (messengers of divine power), and, by that knowledge, participates in the emergence of erotic power. Such a return to heart is a journey from death to life. The journey to life opens him to relationships with others in erotic power.

To have faced our demons is never to forget their power to hurt and never to forget the power to heal that lies in touching brokenheartedness. To heal is to be capable of relationships of erotic power because we have faced our own pain and despair. We are empowered not to be fainthearted in the face of pain because we remember brokenheartedness. We know our capacity to be tempted by the false security of unilateral power. Our need for control lies close to our vulnerability and capacity to be hurt. Hence to exorcise and heal is not to develop amnesia with a nostalgic view of the past or to believe brokenheartedness has been overcome. Exorcism must have *anamnesis*, remembrance of our whole past for the sake of erotic power, which involves touching heart to heart as the wellspring of erotic power. Remembering opens resources for erotic power through our ability to see through brokenheartedness.

Jesus' heartfelt openness to the sacred reality revealed to him in the hearts of others and the willingness of those who seek help to make themselves vulnerable create the space for erotic power to emerge. Erotic power is revealed by the dialectic of the brokenhearted, who reveal the fragility of heart and the necessity for connection, and by Jesus' listening to the brokenhearted, who actively seek him out. Erotic power surfaces as Jesus hears, below the demon noises, an anguished cry for deliverance. Through their mutual touching, Christa/Community is cocreated as a continuing, liberating, redemptive reality.

Healing Suffering: Whole-Making Work

The Gospel therapeutic healings not involving demons highlight another dimension of erotic power. The healing stories are not especially concerned with political domination, with positional power. Instead they deal with social relationships when hierarchical powers are removed—with the nature of relationships as they ought to be lived in Christa/Community.

Healers in Hellenistic culture were understood to possess special powers. Powers so strong that, at times, they emitted an aura or independent mana that unfolded automatically. Extension of the healer's essence, through spittle, especially as condensed breath, or blood, as life force, could carry the healing power. Whether through touching or through his aura and its extensions, Jesus' healing is indicated as the transference of power, which is an understanding of power as something a self possesses. However, as is the case with all seemingly unilateral forms of power, the power made available to all who participate in an event emerges from the relationships involved. Mark hints at the relational nature of healing through the concept of faith, which the afflicted always bring to the healing event.

The function of the healer is not to gain power, but to facilitate the recreation of it. In the sharing process, heart reveals the sacred. Between healer and sufferer something blocks the flow of erotic power, which normatively, should be present. The afflicted are suffering from some sort of brokenheartedness that denies them the capacity to play in the field of erotic power. The flow of power between healer and afflicted represents the touching of heart to heart and the emergence of erotic power. Brokenheartedness takes on a strong social dimension in Elisabeth Schüssler Fiorenza's interpretation of the story of the hemorrhaging woman.[6] This story in Mark 5 follows the exorcism of the demoniac.

The woman's story, according to Schüssler Fiorenza, represents a social reality still experienced by women. In her study of the origins of patriarchy, Gerda Lerner convincingly hinges the roots of male dominance on the control of female sexuality and reproduction. Women's reproductive capacities become support for patriarchy, which uses subordination, rape, and murder to control women's sexual activity and usurps female birthing into male images of creation, ritual bleeding, and birthing. Systems of male dominance teach negative attitudes about women's bodies: their bleeding as polluting, their birthing as problematic, and their genitals as dirty.

With similar attitudes toward women's bodies found in the first century, the healing stories of the hemorrhaging woman and Jairus's daughter demonstrate a vision of what life in the *basileia* ought to be for women, according to Schüssler Fiorenza. The healing of the hemorrhaging woman is placed between the beginning and end of the healing of Jairus's daughter (Mark 5:21–43). The reasons for the two females' ailments are not given. Etiology is unimportant. But the juxtaposition of the two stories, according to Schüssler Fiorenza, creates interlocking meanings.

> As soon as Jesus had returned by boat to the other shore, a great crowd once more gathered round him. While he was by the lake-side, the president of one of the synagogues came up, Jairus by name, and, when he saw him, threw himself down at his feet and pleaded with him. "My little daughter," he said, "is at death's door. I beg you to come and lay your hands on her to cure her and save her life." So Jesus went with him, accompanied by a great crowd which pressed upon him.
>
> Among them was a woman who had suffered from haemorrhages for twelve years; and in spite of long treatment by many doctors, on which she had spent all she had, there had been no improvement; on the contrary, she had grown worse. She had heard what people were saying about Jesus, so she came up from behind in the crowd and touched his cloak; for she said to herself, "If I touch even his clothes, I shall be cured." And there and then the source of her haemorrhages dried up and she knew in herself that she was cured of her trouble. At the same time Jesus, aware that power had gone out of him, turned round in the crowd and asked, "Who touched my clothes?" His disciples said to him, "You see the crowd pressing upon you and yet you ask, 'Who touched me?'." Meanwhile he was looking round to see who had done it. And the woman, trembling with fear when she grasped what had happened to her, came and fell at his feet and told him the whole truth. He said to her, "My daughter, your faith has cured you. Go in peace, free for ever from this trouble." [*New English Bible*, Mark 5: 21–34]

Both females are afflicted with crises associated with the status of women in Greco-Roman and Hebraic society. The adult woman is sick with one of the most polluting signs of female adulthood. The adolescent is on the threshold of a similar curse, puberty. The woman has suffered with bleeding for exactly the same period of time as it has taken Jairus's daughter to reach the official age of puberty and marriageability—twelve years. The woman's hemorrhage is the affliction of adult women in magnified form; she bleeds endlessly and is perpetually polluting. The authorities, the physicians, have left her poor and sick. They cannot help her disease because the ordinary social structures cannot help her. They are part of her problem. We see again in Mark that the usual power of sacred sources and authorities are challenged. She suffers from her very femaleness. The social structures also interfere with Jesus' ability to help her because he is a Jewish man. He is not even able to see her. She is invisible to him, lost in the protective maze of disciples.

The woman is, nonetheless, determined to be whole. She is able to acknowledge, from the depths of herself, her heart, her desperate need to be healed, to be restored to right relationships. Her heart opens the space for erotic power to surface. She summons the courage to violate a patriarchal social taboo. Though an unclean woman, she touches Jesus in public. She comes "up from behind" to touch him, out of his view. In the touching, she is, literally, saved, not just cured in a medical sense, but saved. Her courage in violating a taboo has made her whole.[7]

The text says Jesus felt a power go out of him. What power? One explanation is that an automatic healer's power left him. But since the woman's courage gives evidence of her heart and she already recognizes she is saved, I want to suggest that the woman takes a different power from Jesus. She takes away his patriarchal power as a man. She breaks through the barrier of male privilege and status that separated them. Again, an old hierarchical power in Mark is replaced with a new vision, this time by the woman's action. *Her* action reveals the "*kenosis* of patriarchy." She acts to reveal the brokenheartedness of patriarchy and cocreates Christa/Community.

The woman's courage compels her, despite her fear, to refuse her own exclusion and invisibility. After she knows she has been made whole and could slip invisibly away, Jesus is still bothered by his loss of power. She is frightened at the implications of her deed, but rather than betray her deepest self-affirming self, she presents herself to full view in front of him. The text, which is translated "fell at his feet" (Mark 5:33), can also mean she embraced him. She makes herself visible. From behind, she moves to front, face to face, heart to heart. Only then is Jesus able to see her. Jesus acknowledges her own faith saved her, free forever from her trouble. Her action allows Jesus fuller participation in erotic power, an action later repeated by the Syro-Phoenician woman (Mark 7:24–30) who shatters his view of religious exclusivity. In both cases, when Jesus stands most acutely in a position of exclusive social and religious privilege over another, he is unable or unwilling to help. It is the courageous work of the "other" that shatters his view of power and privilege. That courage challenges the structures of benign paternalism that would give Jesus the power from above to fix the power inequities involved.

> While he was still speaking, a message came from the president's house, "Your daughter is dead; why trouble the Rabbi further?" But Jesus, overhearing the message as it was delivered, said to the president of the

synagogue, "Do not be afraid; only have faith." After this he allowed no one to accompany him except Peter and James and James's brother John. They came to the president's house, where he found a great commotion, with loud crying and wailing. So he went in and said to them, "Why this crying and commotion? The child is not dead; she is asleep"; and they only laughed at him. But after turning all the others out, he took the child's father and mother and his own companions and went in where the child was lying. Then, taking hold of her hand, he said to her, "*Talitha cum,*" which means, "Get up, my child." Immediately the girl got up and walked about—she was twelve years old. At that they were beside themselves with amazement. He gave them strict orders to let no one hear about it, and told them to give her something to eat. [*New English Bible,* Mark 5:35–43]

During the delay caused by the woman's action, the daughter dies. According to Schüssler Fiorenza, bleeding symbolizes death for women because it signifies isolation from the community. The emergence of womanhood for Jairus's daughter has had fatal consequences, but the previous healing event hints at a reality already present. The older woman's courage has removed for Jesus the barrier of patriarchal privilege. He has seen in a new way. Jesus declares the child is only asleep. He seeks to awaken her. Her adult female status is not denied, but affirmed as positive and active. "Immediately the girl got up and walked about—she was twelve years old" (Mark 5:41). Now, with her heart restored, she can play.

The context of the text points beyond personal illness to the social nature of the two women's ailments. Behind the two women stand countless others who are encouraged to have courage and to remove the barriers that exclude them from full participation in the *basileia.* They are images of the removal of death and return to life of all women made invisible by patriarchy. According to Schüssler Fiorenza, the defiling element of womanhood is transformed.

If we use Schüssler Fiorenza's contention that women represent, at least in some of the biblical stories, the marginal in society, the stories of the hemorrhaging woman and Jairus's daughter take on important heuristic meanings as normative statements about relationships within the Christian community. As metaphors of exclusion, the women represent those who have been denied admission to or full participation in the church on the basis of factors over which authorities and experts have no power. The building of barriers against those who threaten entrenched structures of dominance and against those who expose the vulnerability of heart destroys erotic power.

Gender, race, sexual orientation, age, culture, language, physical ability, and all other embodiments of heart that are part of the complex nature of persons and their relationships to life are denied as reasons for exclusion or subordination. The stories call on those who have the power to exclude and oppress others to have a change of heart, to be open to a transformation that empowers them to embrace wholeheartedly the whole and compassionate being.

This social aspect of the story can only make sense if the women are specifically understood in their femaleness under patriarchy. Without the specificity of gender and historical context, the theological implications are lost. The hemorrhaging woman regarded, not in some essential humanness, but in her historical particularity *as a woman*, represents the radical implications of the claiming of heart. As those excluded by structures of unilateral power, the brokenhearted are called to action. We are not called to place our faith in benignly paternalistic powers who will rescue us or protect us from suffering. We are to have faith in our own worth, which empowers us to be healed by each other. Despite fear of the consequences, we are summoned to take heart, to refuse despair, and to act for ourselves and each other. Taking heart creates more healing; it opens new ways of power. Thus those who follow in later generations will be given life, increasing the possibilities for erotic power, just as the woman's act touches Jairus's daughter.

The interlocking of the women's stories also makes them renderable as images of one person. In acknowledging her own heart, the woman is returned to the play space of the child through her faith. As a woman, she has sought a source to remove her isolation and restore her to wholeness. In doing so, she creates the possibility for the playful child in her to come back to life. She is restored to erotic power by her insistence on heart to heart relationships with someone unable to see her. In the joining of the two stories, the two aspects of one woman are returned to the erotic space of woman/child. This joining, this mediation of opposites, is also symbolized, according to Malbon, in the use of Jairus's house. He is a ruler of a synagogue, a sacred place, but the healing takes place in his house, a profane place. It is as if the conventionally sacred realm had become inadequate to contain this new power of healing.

In Mark 6, Jesus' conflict with the synagogue results in his absence from synagogues for the rest of Mark. If Christians had been expelled from the synagogue by the time of Mark's writing, this transposition of space may reflect the church's attempt to integrate its earlier work in synagogues with the reality of its later work in houses. Whatever the background, Malbon contends, the breakdown of the conventional understanding of space in Mark brings a new reality:

> By the close of the Gospel of Mark, no architectural space functions in
> its normal, expected way any longer. A house is no longer a family
> dwelling but has become a gathering place for the new community,
> replacing the rejected and rejecting synagogue . . . all [places] are,
> according to Mark's Gospel, witnesses to the breakdown of the sacred
> and the profane and the breakthrough to a new reality. [1986, p. 140]

The final mediation of space takes place in the passion narrative, which will
be discussed in the following chapter.

The profoundly relational nature of heart and its cocreation of erotic power
is strongly suggested in the exorcism and healing stories. Heart does not lie
exclusively with Jesus. In Mark 6, the text states explicitly that Jesus is
unable alone to work any miracles. Miracles require heart. "He could work
no miracle there, except that he put his hands on a few sick people and healed
them; and he was taken aback by their want of faith" (Mark 6:6). Immediately after his failure, Jesus sends "the Twelve" in pairs to exorcise and
heal. "They drove out many devils, and many sick people they anointed with
oil and cured" (Mark 6:13). Hence Jesus begins his work by calling helpers
and then sends them out to expand the field of erotic power, which he cannot
do alone.

The new power revealed in this first section of Mark reverses old expectations. In stories of unilateral power—demons, a stormy sea, poverty and
hunger, disease, and religious and political authority—when Jesus would
appear to be impotent, with no official power, the divine power to heal and
ease suffering is revealed. The unexpected and new power is participated in
by Jesus, but it is not his alone because in several stories in which someone
else is victim structurally to Jesus' unilateral power, for example, the Syro-
Phoenician and hemorrhaging women, Jesus represents the old power. The
point is not Jesus' sole possession of power, but the revelation of a new
understanding of power that connects members of the community. The
power reversal comes from those perceived as weak who reveal the divine way
of power, erotic power.

The Work of Erotic Power

The spread of erotic power creates excitement in those touched by it. The
brokenhearted restored to wholeness make Christa/Community visible and
spread Jesus' fame. The presence of such heart disturbs Herod, the ultimate
symbol of heartless, hierarchical power. But Herod's sources seem unable to
pinpoint the exact person responsible for the unrest he sees, disturbing him

even more. For they are seeking in one source the possessor of unilateral power and misunderstand the nature of this new power.

Later in Mark, after the first feeding of the multitudes, the walking on water, many healings, the second feeding story, and the transfiguration, John asks Jesus what to do about outsiders who, using the name of Jesus, have the same liberating and healing effect on people. The disciples, as representatives of those who misunderstand Jesus' power, want to stop any unauthorized competition. Jesus says not to interfere. "For he who is not against us is on our side" (Mark 9:40). Thus ends the section of Mark in which we are introduced to this new way of power. The emergence of this erotic power has been the work of Christa/Community through the presence of heart.

Because heart works in the play space of erotic power, the specific acts required to heal vary from context to context. No one healing image can include every particular situation and no single interpretation of the texts is final. Sources of suffering vary with time and space. The Markan text is not concerned with diagnosis, blame, and guilt. Rather, it proclaims that sickness, political oppression, poverty, and death should not have final say. It proclaims that erotic power as Spirit-Sophia dwelling in the Christa/Community is revealed through the presence of heart, and it can heal brokenheartedness.[8]

Erotic power does not compel us to believe exclusive ideologies or to be loyal to a particular image of deity from which we derive hope, authority, or power. Nor should it lead us to trust in the power of benign paternalism. Rather, through the heart within ourselves, through the image of erotic power in our very being, we are led to liberation and to the miraculous recreation of Christa/Community by our heartfelt connection to others. Erotic power creates life in the midst of the ambiguity of existence by making heart possible. Passion and compassion are alive in the touching of hearts. Brokenheartedness that is embraced exorcises oppression and heals pain by revealing openings for the work of erotic power. The play space of erotic power gives all it touches life and hope.

·5·

The Gospel of Mark: Erotic Power in the Shadows

The Gospel of Mark does not end on an unambiguous note of celebration. It ends in conflict and death, with only the smallest flash of hope. Chapters 11–16 focus on suffering and on the true disciple as one who is willing to suffer. The original disciples who had participated so enthusiastically in gaining fame fled. Jesus dies believing he has been abandoned by God. All who remain at his death to hold any relationship together are three named women and several unnamed others. Mary of Magdala and Mary the mother of Joseph are the only ones to see the location of his tomb. The two Marys and Salome are so frightened by their vision of the resurrection that the text says they told no one.

The exorcisms and healings, which reveal erotic power as the hallmark of the Christa/Community, all but disappear as the shadow of Jesus' cross looms large on the horizon. The earlier joy of erotic power appears to have gone underground. Images of suffering—of picking up one's cross, of losing one's self to gain self, and of coming persecutions—seep up through the angry cracks of the cleansing of the temple, the cursing of the fig tree, the parable of the tenants, and the arguments with Scribes and Sadducees. The images of suffering and anger culminate in the apocalyptic visions of Mark 13 which immediately precede the passion narrative.

Schüssler Fiorenza sees in Mark 8–10 an important transition between the two parts of the Gospel, as it shifts the meaning of discipleship from the disciples' misunderstanding of it as glory to its true nature as the experience of persecution and suffering out of solidarity with the marginal. The sayings on true discipleship are preceded and succeeded by the healing of blind persons, the second of which emphasizes the role of faith in discipleship. The healings of the blind imply that the church must open its eyes to the truth of discipleship revealed in the second part of Mark. Schüssler Fiorenza sees these texts as setting a tension with and implying a rejection of the christ-ology in the first part of Mark (pp. 316–319).

In the discussion below, I will show how the two parts of Mark interact with each other and how the second presupposes the first part. Hence the healings and exorcisms, as they reveal a new understanding of divine power, are not rejected in the second part. Instead, they are deepened and more profoundly affirmed by the suffering depicted in the passion narrative. That suffering highlights poignantly how difficult trust in erotic power is in the face of oppressive systems and how crucial that trust is to a community's survival.

The Shadows of Salvific Death

Christological statements rest upon claims about the character of human existence and doctrines of divine incarnation with corollary views of how our broken human existence is redeemed by divine power. Various soteriologies, or doctrines of salvation, have proclaimed that the death of Jesus is salvific, a soteriology that feminists such as Mary Daly call necrophilic. We are encouraged to glorify death. The death of Jesus becomes a way to life that transcends our maternal birth by rebirth through the father's grace. Jesus' death is asserted to be the ultimate sign of self-sacrifice and divine self-giving, and a symbol of the willingness of true believers to sacrifice them-selves out of devotion to a higher authority or will. His death is seen as a death for others, a cosmic event in which the death of God in Christ becomes the death of death. In taking on the burdens of all who desert him and deserve to die, Jesus dies in their stead. His resurrection is interpreted as the sign of divine triumphal powers that vindicate Jesus as the true messiah.

The spiritualization of life and death results in the rejection of nature, the body, and physical birth. In *Sexism and God-Talk* Ruether believes male consciousness focuses its misogynist energy in a world-fleeing spirituality.

> To be born in the flesh is already to be subject to change, which is a devolution toward decay and death. Only by extricating mind from matter . . . can one prepare for the salvific escape out of the realm of corruptibility to eternal spiritual life. All that sustains physical life— sex, eating, reproduction, even sleep—comes to be seen as sustaining the realm of "death," against which a mental realm of consciousness has been abstracted as the realm of "true life." Women, as representatives of

sexual reproduction and motherhood, are the bearers of death, from which male spirit must flee to "light and life." [pp. 79 80]

Ruether asserts this rejection of nature continues today in the scientific attempt to control nature.

The passion narratives have been interpreted as the story of a heroic savior who faced his enemies alone and unaided. Jesus' death becomes the battle of unilateral powers. In returning Jesus to life, divine unilateral action conquers the power of sin and death. Because the resurrection did not cause the downfall of powers of political oppression, the official church made the meaning of his death spiritual and other-worldly. Hope became a hope in personal salvation through the death and resurrection of one heroic, divinely appointed person. Only a transcendent and powerful deity can save us, for all human power has failed.

This passive helplessness is the alter ego of the egocentric, destructive masculine self. This emphasis on helplessness balances the sins of hubris, but finds no path to empower the heart. In *From a Broken Web* Catherine Keller asserts that cowardice and a deadly passivity lie below the surface of the aggressive androcentric ego, which is unable to face the monsters lurking beneath its fear of intimacy, and which must use a mirror to see the monsters created by its denial of relationships, "killing 'by reflection' what one is too cowardly to face" (p. 63). This mirroring occurs through the death of Jesus who must function to face our judgment for us and protect us from the punishing face of the father.

The resurrection was used as proof of a transcendent deity's power to save helpless humanity and to deliver life in the midst of death. When all human effort failed, when Jesus died alone and abandoned, his heavenly father restored Jesus to life, removing the guilt of his followers' betrayal. Because only the father had the power to create and take life, humanity was called to receive and witness to divine power in the crucifixion and resurrection. The resurrection became the focus of hope in a spiritualized and other-worldly life. It contained the promise of life for individuals beyond the sphere of the world of sin. All the saved are united by this one promise against the powers of death. The promise of life is only granted by God through Jesus. Humanity is helpless, except for the capacity to believe and hope.

Schüssler Fiorenza takes Paul to task for his version of soteriology which universalizes Jesus' death.

Paul does not understand the crucifixion in concrete political terms as the outcome of the conflict of Jesus' vision with that of the established power of this world. This fact has far-reaching consequences for Pauline theology, which attempts to spell out the newness of Christian life in the context of history in order to prevent the evaporation of the Christian vision into a mere dream or fanciful ideology. However, whereas Jesus died on the cross because of his deviance from, and opposition to, the religious-social order of his time, the cross of Jesus becomes, in Paul's thought, so universalized that it applies to all human frailty and mortality. [p. 187]

Behind most soteriological perspectives lies the assumption that Jesus' death was necessary. Either some divine teleology requires it or human sin inflicts it. Even Henry Nelson Wieman, who develops a thoroughly relational perspective in discussing Jesus and his community, speaks of Jesus' death as necessary.

> We have told of the life of Jesus. The death of Jesus is equally important. Indeed, it is indispensable to our salvation. So long as Jesus lived, the creative event was bound to limits and confined by obstructions which would have prevented it from bringing salvation to man if Jesus had not been crucified. . . . Before the Resurrection, the disciples of Jesus were unable to undergo the transformations of creative interchange beyond the bounds of their cultural heritage.[1]

Wieman draws continuity from discontinuity, connectedness from disconnection, life from death. The human tendency to control an event blocks its creative purposes, and it took Jesus' death to shatter the illusions of control implied by his presence. Wieman claims the bounds of cultural relativity were broken by Jesus' death because the concept of messiah had to be reconceived.

Wieman's need to disparage cultural heritage as too restrictive of the salvific Christian message places a negative connotation on the rich complexities of experience that constitute cultural heritage. His statement also carries implications of an anti-Jewish supersessionism in which the Judaism of Jesus and his community is seen as too narrow to contain the higher universalism of Christian salvation. Wieman assumes that persons must transcend cultural heritage to find a higher more universal truth, which is not limited to a particular religious tradition. His unitive vision of human good, which he says must emerge from connections, is contradicted by his statement about Jesus' death. I believe we come to any understanding about reality through cultural heritage and our encounter with others who are different from us. The more complex our world of connections, the richer is the world from which we draw concepts for understanding reality. The world of first-century Judaism and the community of those who lived and worked with Jesus already represent some of the intersections of cultures present in Galilee and Jerusalem in the first century. Moving beyond the limitedness of a too narrow culture comes not from transcending that culture but expanding its capacity for inclusiveness through connection. In that transmutation, our cultural heritage is enriched and expanded.

The important point is not that Jesus' death had to happen, but that the community responded to it from its own cultural heritage by maintaining connections within its community, connections from which emerged both a stronger need for power as control and a creative response to tragedy. Jesus' death may indeed have shattered any illusions the disciples had about control. Control is one problematic element in patriarchal societies, but it is not necessarily transcended by tragic disconnection. Jesus' death also produced betrayal, defensiveness, rationalization, and fear. It may have been that his death caused a more defensive and controlling reaction from his community than would have happened if he had not been executed. The shift away from control comes through healing and self-awareness.

If we begin with different assumptions that see connectedness as the inclusive category, we can understand that disconnection comes from our awareness of connection, that discontinuities are a part of continuities, and that death, in its many forms, is a part of life. We can begin to see that through erotic power we come to greater comprehensions of reality and truth. In a relational universe in which causality is not deterministic and linear and in which the creative responses of the present create possibilities for the future, it is impossible to claim, as Wieman does, that any particular event was necessary. In fact, the tendency to make claims of necessity, especially about events as complicated as a person's political execution, limits our capacity to understand the range of possibilities for creative responses to events. Creative purposes serve and emerge from our deepest connectedness to the largest whole possible.

Jesus' death was tragic, but it neither had to happen nor was part of a divine plan for salvation. Jesus may even, in desperation, have provoked his death because of his own ideas about such plans, but it was not an event necessary to reveal erotic power or save humankind. The brokenheartedness revealed in his death is created by the political systems of patriarchal society and was neither inevitable nor necessary. Such evidence of brokenheartedness does call us, however, to take heed and to understand.

Persons we love evoke our compassion, and to claim anyone's premature death is necessary leads us to thinking suffering is something we cannot protest. To make claims that any person's tragic, painful death is divinely willed or necessary for others to be saved mutes our ability to be angry about unnecessary suffering. Such claims dull the acuteness of our caring. We lose our rage at injustice and our passionate desire to eliminate the structures that produce brokenheartedness. We lose heart.

Courage in the Face of Shadows

In times of extreme political tyranny, to challenge structures of authority is always to risk death, but the point of the risk is not to invite death. The risk is a profound affirmation of the possibility of life beyond oppression. Jesus' death was a political event in which Jesus attempted to force a confrontation with the Romans, an interpretation put forward by many liberation theologians. His acts in the passion narrative are acts of impassioned commitment, even perhaps of rage, rather than acts of self-sacrifice. His political acts are not acts in which he chose to die. He chose to live for himself and the people he loved by challenging the oppressive powers that destroyed what he loved. His risk is a commitment to solidarity with those crushed by oppressive powers and to the expectation that justice must prevail.

We can see in Jesus' cleansing of the temple (Mark 11:15–18) an act of civil disobedience and an example of how Jesus' passion became extremely dangerous. The clarity of such anger and commitment can be an illuminating revelation and inspiration for similar courage to those who recognize it. Acts of civil disobedience sometimes are. In *Has God Rejected His People?* Clark Williamson claims that Jesus' act of outrage was too much of an affront to the Romans to go unpunished.[2] But Jesus' death must have been a disappointing conclusion to those who expected a triumphant messiah and who could not see in his anger a mirror of their own passionate commitment to liberation and wholeness. Nor could they see in his death a warning of the consequences of defying authority. Instead they made him an authority, a salvific protector. His special status to them was as a substitute for their punishment, for they could not give up their need to worship hierarchical powers. They began to think his death was demanded by a power who willed it to protect them, a divine power mightier than Rome.

In *To Change the World* Rosemary Ruether discusses Jesus' death as a political act and points to the hope that persons committed to liberation can draw from the tragedy of Jesus' death.

> The meaning of the cross, of redemptive suffering, also appears in a different light for those who suffer and are killed as part of the struggle for justice. Too often Christians have treated the suffering Christ as some kind of cosmic legal transaction with God to pay for the sins of humanity, as though anyone's sufferings and death could actually "pay for" others' sins! Christ's cross is used to inculcate a sense of masochistic guilt, unworthiness and passivity in Christians. . . . To accept and endure evil is regarded as redemptive. . . . Solidarity with the poor and with those who suffer does not mean justifying these evils, but struggling to overcome them. As one struggles against evil, one also risks suffering and becomes vulnerable to retaliation and violence to those who are intent on keeping the present system intact. . . . But risking suffering and even death on behalf of a new society, we also awaken hope. [pp. 27–28]

Ruether discusses how extreme oppression produces a profound memory of tragic death. However, the memory itself reduces the sting of death. The poor and oppressed, in participating in their own liberation, understand the web of connections that sustain their own lives and the ones who have gone before. The connections give them hope that the powers of death can be broken.

The Gospel of Mark refuses to sentimentalize death. At his death Jesus pays the severest penalty that oppressive powers can inflict. His death is evidence of the power of patriarchy to crush life. In dying he reveals the power of the brokenhearted. He cannot save himself alone. His status as victim of brokenheartedness is a shadow throughout the entire Gospel story. Immediately before his death, the Twelve who would eventually desert Jesus are shown still expecting a triumphant messiah. But Jesus did not defeat Rome with the armies of God. Instead he died in the hands of Rome. The shock of defeat and loss of messianic hopes seems to have been profound for those disciples who expected deliverance by an omnipotent God and a unilaterally powerful messiah. These disciples are still tempted to worship hierarchical power. They have not fully understood the way of erotic power or the vulnerability of heart. In their betrayal, the fleeing disciples felt guilty and understood Jesus' death as deserved by all, as Ruether mentions. They saw Jesus' death as a death for them, so that they might live.

The Markan view of Jesus' death is not that he should suffer alone, but that all true disciples are called to risk a commitment, as a caring community, to the promise of the *basileia* as a domination-free community. This call was answered by some of the disciples. They are found under the cross risking their lives and safety having left everything to be on the way of the new power, even to the bitterness of the cross. The call to discipleship is a call to courage in the face of the shadow of the cross. With such courage, life in the midst of death surfaces through connection.

The Circle that Embraces Shadows

The passion narrative is incomplete at Jesus' death. The illumination of the sacred is incomplete, for the relationships of Christa/Community appear nearly severed, at least for "the Twelve." However, the Gospel continues to hint at the healing power of Christa/Community through the presence of the women. They are identified as the disciples who have participated in a community of healing and empowerment and who take courage in the power of that community. This presence has already been revealed as a foreshadowing in the story of the anointing at Bethany that is the central focus of Schüssler Fiorenza's *In Memory of Her*. This woman at Bethany has opened the circle of healing that is completed in the return of the women to the grave.

> Jesus was at Bethany, in the house of Simon the leper. As he sat at table, a woman came in carrying a small bottle of very costly perfume, pure oil of nard. She broke it open and poured the oil over his head. Some of those present said to one another angrily, "Why this waste? The perfume might have been sold for thirty pounds and the money given to the poor"; and they turned upon her with fury. But Jesus said, "Let her alone. Why must you make trouble for her? It is a fine thing she has done for me. You have the poor among you always, and you can help them whenever you like; but you will not always have me. She has done what lay in her power; she is beforehand with anointing my body for burial. I tell you this: wherever in all the world the Gospel is proclaimed, what she has done will be told as her memorial." [*New English Bible*, Mark 14: 3–9]

Schüssler Fiorenza interprets this story as messianic: a messiah was proclaimed by being anointed with oil. The Hebrew *messiah* means anointed one, as does the Greek *Christos*. The use of oil made the act a messianic one, indicating Jesus' special status in his community, a status given to him by that community. Anointing with oil also carries healing connotations. Mark 6 makes reference to the disciples who anointed with oil in their mission as healers. Oils were used as part of the healing arts. The woman at Bethany uses oil of nard, an unguent, whose expense highlights the importance of her act. Healing through the applications of unguents can be seen in this story, especially since the anointing is connected to burial and to women's responsibility for preparing bodies for burial.[3]

Various oils were healer's substances, used in folk medicine to mediate divine miraculous powers from the healer to the afflicted. Oil was also used to prepare bodies for burial. Effective substances were often called "hands of the gods." In both its messianic and healing functions, oil represented the giving of divine power to the anointed. At Bethany messianic power is joined with healing power and with untimely and brutal death, the ultimate brokenheartedness. Jesus will become the suffering one who has already been healed into a circle of erotic power. The image of impending death in Mark 14:8 places the anointing in the sphere of a life-and-death struggle. While Jesus is not physically sick, he is about to enter the realm of death, but he has been prepared for death by the woman. By her labor, she moves him into another realm from which he will emerge reborn. She has placed her healing hand upon his head, making another anointing at the tomb unnecessary. The oil symbolizes, in this interpretation, the continuity and preciousness of erotic power.

This woman, as a woman, represents the revelatory and healing power of heart. She becomes prophet and healer by her act as representative of the Christa/Community that would survive Jesus' death and witness his resurrection. She anoints Jesus. Her unorthodox behavior raises objections from the disciples, objections which Jesus rejects. Her action is bold, political, and indicative of the special place some women have in Mark's narrative. Among the disciples, they often represent those who best understand Jesus' vision of *basileia* and his revelation of a new power.

Jesus' brokenhearted death is not the end of the story because the woman had already affirmed the erotic power in their community, a community that would survive his death. Her anointing symbolizes a circle of response that enfolds Jesus in loving care and that is, in the caring, able to integrate his death and suffering even as the community is tempted to deny their reality or glorify them. The anointing, as a foreshadowing of healing and resurrection, transferred the role of healer and healed. This reversal in Mark parallels other themes of reversal in which the unexpected power relation is undercut by its opposite. Divine power, unleashed by the reversal, flows between the woman and Jesus. This healing act buoys the coming trial with an undercurrent of connection. Divine power remained in the community of those who healed and ministered to each other.

If we read Mark as a whole, we can see how the text mediates the destructive potential of suffering and death with its introduction of erotic power in the healed community. The disciples who have been set off on the new way—the journey into the territories of erotic power—bind the revelation of erotic power in the first part of Mark to the suffering in the second part. These disciples were part of the Christa/Community of Galilee, the community of exorcism and healing. They went with Jesus to Jerusalem. Their community after Jesus' death takes heart through their remembrance of exorcism and healing as the revelation of a new power, through the resurrection as a witness against the finality of a single member's death, and through the continuing work of Christa/Community. These disciples sustain a connectedness that encompasses suffering. That vision began with their own empowerment in Galilee but has, in this passion narrative, moved to the anointing at Bethany and is set on its way at the empty tomb. Following the death of Jesus, his community began to shape its memories, integrating all that happened to it, and to reformulate its task as witness to and interpreters of what had happened.

From Jesus' community, the only witnesses of Jesus' death to which all four Gospels attest were the women. Schüssler Fiorenza contends the women were essential as witnesses. Jesus does not die totally abandoned, though he is described as feeling godforsaken. The divine erotic power illuminated through Christa/Community in Galilee and the woman at Bethany is sustained through Jesus' death by those who watch him die and mark his burial site. They represent those who have experienced the liberating, empowering presence of erotic power. The women also represent a caring, patient presence that can be wounded but not denied. They return later to the grave to repeat the anointing. Though frightened, they do not lose heart and leave Jesus alone. In their patriarchal time and context, the women find erotic power, self-possession, and hope. They are not perfect disciples; they simply persist with heart in the midst of brokenheartedness. They are the testimony that connection is essential to erotic power. The women at the cross mourn, are afraid, and yet persist with the care at Jesus' tomb that they knew before his death.

The death of Jesus reveals the brokenheartedness of patriarchy. His dying is a testimony to the powers of oppression. It is neither salvific nor essential. It is tragic. The suffering of Jesus reveals the reality of brokenheartedness found in the possessed, oppressed, sick, and wounded in the exorcisms and healings. Jesus in his death calls attention to brokenheartedness. Just as the suffering of those who went before him and those who come after him has done, his suffering compels us not to despair but to remember him and all others who suffer and to seek erotic power by our own action.

That seeking is called forth honestly. The costs of such commitment and the realities of brokenheartedness are presented in Mark without nostalgia. Throughout the Gospel, the power of honest memory becomes a way to integrate the tensions and paradoxes of expectations to glory and the reality of suffering. Mark does not give us a rosy picture of the origins of the Christa/Community. Ambivalence and fear appear through misunderstandings and failures of faith in the community despite miraculous wonders. This embracing of failure presents a forgiving picture of the cost of discipleship even as it warns of the risks involved. The joy of liberation in exorcism and the wonder of wholeness from healing are not illusions but remembrances. Schüssler Fiorenza lumps the whole first part of Mark together, including the miracle stories, as a christology of glory that is replaced by the christology of suffering and death of the second part. However, I believe the glory and triumph sought by the disciples who misunderstand Jesus' power is not the same power revealed by the miracle stories. I believe the remembrances of exorcism and healing are not rejected in favor of suffering and death. Rather, the potential of erotic power to liberate and make whole is glimpsed enough to empower the community to withstand and integrate tragedy. That glimpse makes Mark's call to wholehearted discipleship a commitment to a real, heartfelt expectation, not to a nostalgic yearning for a forgotten past or gossamer hope for a utopian future.

This forgiving and empowering *anamnesis* is vividly depicted in Doris Lessing's *The Four-Gated City*, the last in her Children of Violence series of novels. After a terrifying, grim cataclysm that destroys the civilized world, Lessing describes a saving remnant: the children of violence who are compassionate and nonviolent. But these children are not salvific because of naiveté or innocence. They are salvific because they remember honestly, without nostalgia, the truth of the violence of human history. These children possess a dangerous historical memory, a memory of the destroyer. This memory does not succumb to, but transforms the destroyer through the children's wholeness of vision and their ability to care for each other. They are an incandescent healing power emerging from ashes.

This dangerous memory of destruction, produced by the Markan witnesses to the crucifixion who continue to care for each other, also produces healing. Their *anamnesis* provides the honest memory that refuses to ignore the terrorizing and afflictive power of patriarchal empires determined to destroy; in the midst of that memory, they will not let life go.

Visions That Light the Way

The disciples of the Christa/Community at the cross provide the dangerous memory. They transform the defeat of death into a wholeness of vision in the midst of pain and sorrow. Even in the midst of brokenheartedness, they refuse to give up on erotic power. When Jesus could no longer be with them, they brought him back through memory and a visionary-ecstatic image of resurrection. Despite the brutalness of death under oppression, the community of faithful disciples restores erotic power and the hope of wholeness for their community by not letting go of their relationships to each other and not letting Jesus' death be the end of their community.

The resurrection of an abandoned Jesus is a meaningless event. The resurrection comes through the witnesses who saw him die, marked his grave in sorrow, and returned to anoint him. These witnesses refused to let death defeat them. In taking heart they remembered his presence and affirmed divine power among them. The resurrection provided a way for Jesus to continue to live in them, and for them to live with and for each other. Their stubborn witness that oppressive powers will not have the last word—their refusal to give up their love for each other and their healing acts of remembrance—give meaning to the resurrection as a profound affirmation of this life, of the lives of those who have gone before and of the right to justice of those who live here and now, who cry out for deliverance and healing.

As an historically verifiable event, the resurrection defies our sense of that which can be scientifically accepted. But if we can see it as evidence of the presence of the magic of play space, its ecstatic, visionary quality is a powerful metaphor for connection. In nonscientific cultures, trances and dreamlike, visionary experiences take on a reality our culture often prefers to relegate to the world of psychological disorders or imagination. Regardless of their ontological status, the actuality of such magical experiences can heal and transform. They give testimony of the capacity of the heart to heal when it is allowed to give full play to the depths of pain in sorrow and memory.

Nelle Morton in her powerful essay "The Goddess as Metaphoric Image" describes the impact of such a visionary resurrection experience in which the sacred power of wholeness is revealed to her.[4] Morton gives herself to a sense of weakness she decides not to fight off, a depression caused by a rare blood disease. She begins by calling up an image of the Goddess who brings to her an image of her dead mother. Her mother apologizes for teaching her negative attitudes toward her female bodily functions and tells her to love the misshapen blood cells that manage to keep her alive. In that moment of the acceptance of her woundedness, Morton's depression is lifted.

> I jumped from my chair and kissed her on the mouth, which she had never allowed us to do because of a lung disease she feared she might transmit to us. But in that kiss I had all the loving hugs she had ever given me. Then she disappeared. [p. 163]

With the disappearance, a spider who spins a cloth, the Goddess, and her mother dissolve into her. She feels made whole.

A similar visionary experience happened to me. When my mother died of a disfiguring and painful cancer in 1983, I found myself so depressed that I could barely function at work. I decided one evening to give in to the depression. I wrote a letter to my mother into which I poured my anger at her for all the wrong things I thought she had done and for all the hurts she had inflicted. As I raged and wept in the deepest parts of myself, I suddenly found myself writing about all the wonderful things she had given me, and everything I would miss because she was gone.

Spent from anger and grief, I lay quietly on the floor, eyes open. I felt, more than heard, a wind at the open doorway to the hall and saw my mother, whole and healed, float into the room toward me. Parallel to my body and several feet above it, she looked into my eyes and said, "It's all right." Her toes touched mine and she entered my body through my feet. I felt a euphoric, peaceful energy return to me. I knew I was going to be all right after that, and I have been.

I have described my experience to others who report their own visions in relation to depression, grief, sickness, loss, and sorrow. The play space of trance and mythic images is rich ground for healing visions. It gives us the capacity to reach the illuminating depths of erotic power. As Morton states,

> I began to see more clearly how we act out of images rather than concepts, especially in crisis situations. . . . The context out of which the [metaphoric] movement emerges depends first on our being present

> to it. The movement that is the metaphoric process, including its end
> surprise, can only be followed and observed, and that depends on intu-
> ition, imagination, and open flexibility in which there is involvement
> and participation on the part of the "pursuer or observer." [pp. 165,170]

These experiences make sense of the resurrection experience of the women
at Jesus' tomb. They are the gifts of heart and cannot be willed into existence. They happen serendipitously as miracles of erotic power, when fullness
of heart—of pain, of fear, of anger, of sorrow, and of joy—can be embraced.
The visions pour through open hearts as a life-giving, wonderful grace, a
wondrous surprise. As bearers of the vision of resurrection, the women at
Jesus' tomb replace the disciples accompanying Jesus at the beginning of his
journey.[5]

The empty tomb, in Malbon's structuralist analysis, represents the final
step before the mediation of all the oppositions that characterize Mark's
Gospel. The tomb, a cleft in an opening that emerges from deep in the
earth—the usual symbol of ultimate chaos—is transposed with the holy
mountain, the usual symbol of divine revelation and power. The Gospel
continually transposes expected relationships of sacred and profane, powerful
and weak. Jesus, who has no final location, is always on the move between
places.

> In this is the mediation, the transformation: Jesus "who was crucified"
> is going to Galilee before them, going where they must go—home—to
> begin life anew, to reorder the chaos. As those who followed Jesus "on
> the road" to Jerusalem were amazed and afraid (10:32), so too those who
> will follow him on the road to Jerusalem to Galilee are amazed and
> afraid. [1986, p. 165–66]

The mediation, the connections between worlds, involves Markan spatial
images in the dynamic movement of the new way. That way, the journey into
the territories of erotic power, can be frightening. The women are described
as fleeing in fear. But their flight is already part of the journey and that
journey is also amazing.

While afraid and temporarily silent, the women, who by conventional
standards, appear powerless, are already journeying in the new territories of
erotic power through the power of their vision. As Malbon states:

> It is no wonder those who stand at the beginning of this way, whether
> the Markan women at the empty tomb or the Markan readers, are amazed

and afraid. Mediation of ORDER and CHAOS is not made easy by Jesus who was crucified and is on the way to Galilee—just possible. [1986, p. 164]

The description of the women's fear allows the hearers of this text to understand the cost of true discipleship. At the same time they know that fear did not stop the community's commitment.

Schüssler Fiorenza contends that Spirit-Sophia-Shekinah is an important theological image of the church's experience of divine presence after the resurrection. The experience of the power of the Spirit is basic for the survival of the Christian missionary movement. The God/dess of this movement is the One who did not leave Jesus in the power of death but raised him "in power" so that he becomes "a life-giving Spirit" (p. 184). The *basileia* is not proclamation, "mere talk" (1 Cor. 4:20) but power that fills all who are "in Christ." The community understood itself to be filled with the divine and gracious Spirit that generates life through living persons. This life force seeks to transform time and history and is present in the resurrected Christa/Community that reveals the living presence of Spirit-Sophia. She is erotic power, the Heart of the Universe. The spiritual presence allows the community to reclaim their heart in mythic-metaphorical form, even in the midst of brokenheartedness. The God/dess of this movement who raised Jesus "in power" is the source of the erotic power which they recreated and which sustained them all along. The Christa/Community incarnated and incarnates the power which restores heart.

The marginal and afflicted represent living people who seek liberation and healing. They symbolize life under patriarchy in the first century. The Gospel of Mark witnesses to the belief that divine power could heal and give life through those who do not lose heart. Erotic power is not brought about by faith in a past salvation, but in the healing deeds of the church as the community of heart, of courage, and of hope—as the incarnate presence of Spirit-Sophia. In Jesus' death and resurrection the church focuses its ability to heal life through erotic power. The living Christa/Community reveals the presence of this Spirit.

The resurrection of Jesus is a powerful image of the need for solidarity among and with victims of oppressive powers. The resurrection affirms that no one person alone can overcome brokenness. Each of us lives in each other in Christa/Community. In caring for each other and in passionately affirming erotic power, we struggle on our journey to create spaces for it to flourish. In standing in solidarity with all who suffer, we must be willing to confront and feel deeply the tragic loss of all who suffer and die and to be empowered to act, even when afraid. Guided by heart, we must travel with each other and remember all who have gone before. By embracing and healing heart, our willingness not to allow brokenheartedness to continue sets us on the way of erotic power.

Epilogue

Journeying by Heart

The remembrance of Jesus' death is a call to decision and action. The Gospel of Mark insists that those who would travel in the territories of erotic power must risk living their new vision. This risk is the process of being on the way, not to a goal at the end of history or time, but always on the journey of expectation that comes from the courage of living by heart. The church claimed the defeat of death by placing salvation in spiritualized form and went on to reproduce unilateral forms of power in its own systems and theology, blaspheming erotic power. The death of Jesus, remembered in its complexity in Mark, provides us with evidence that our reliance on unilateral powers will cause us to betray our own original grace and perpetuate suffering and destruction. No one heroic or divine deed will defeat oppressive powers and death-delivering systems. We cannot rely on one past event to save our future. No almighty power will deliver us from evil. With each minute we wait for such rescue, more die.

The power that gives and sustains life does not flow from a dead and resurrected savior to his followers. Rather, the community sustains life-giving power by its memory of its own brokenheartedness and of those who have suffered and gone before and by its members being courageously and redemptively present to all. In doing so, the community remains Christa/ Community and participates in the life-giving flow of erotic power. No one person or group exclusively reveals it or incarnates it. In thinking that a single person, a savior, or even one group can save us, we mistake the crest of a wave for the vast sea churning beneath it.

Jesus is like the whitecap on a wave. The whitecap is momentarily set off from the swell that is pushing it up, making us notice it. But the visibility of the whitecap, which draws our attention, rests on the enormous pushing power of the sea—of its power to push with life-giving labor, to buoy up all lives, and to unite diverse shores with its restless energy. That sea becomes monstrous and chaotically destructive when we try to control it, and its life-giving power is denied. Jesus' power lies with the great swells of the ocean without which the white foam is not brought to visibility. To understand the fullness of erotic power we must look to the ocean which is the whole and compassionate being, including ourselves.

No one else can help us avoid our own pain. No one else can stop the suffering of brokenheartedness in our world but our own courage and willingness to act in the midst of the awareness of our own fragility. No one else can die for us or bring justice, liberation, and healing. The refusal to give up on ourselves and our willingness to struggle with brokenheartedness, involve us in healing the powers of destruction, which must be taken into our circle of remembrance and healing if we are to understand and love the whole of life. Our heartfelt action, not alone, but in the fragile, resilient interconnections we share with others, generates the power that makes and sustains life. There, in the erotic power of heart, we find the sacred mystery that binds us in loving each other fiercely in the face of suffering and pain and that empowers our witness against all powers of oppression and destruction.

In facing the ambivalent realities of our own lives and of the patriarchal societies in which we live, we are led to heal ourselves and each other. In the self-acceptance and wholeness that come with healing, we are empowered to live by heart, to reach out to each other and to the whole aching and groaning cosmos in acts of honest remembrance and heartfelt connection. We are called to find the courage to face the destructive forces of brokenheartedness in solidarity with all those who suffer.

The territories of erotic power have few guides. The journey is dangerous. To be speaking of vulnerability, intimacy, and interdependence in the late twentieth century may seem like folly. The militaristic structures of patriarchy seem determined to rush our planet headlong into the throes of a final all-encompassing nuclear death or an economic and environmental burnout, a slow, sizzling extinction. What possible power can grace, love, gentleness, and compassion have to stop the machines of unilateral power? In *Gyn/Ecology* Mary Daly notes that the believers in the apocalyptic visions of patriarchal religion seem determined to literalize biblical metaphors of divine destruction. Because we have believed in a divine being capable of such destructive power, we have made ourselves in that image. The false security of polarizing the world into friends and enemies and good and evil and wanting to destroy what frightens us is poignantly revealed in the mutually assured destruction of a nuclear war. The need to deny our physical birth and connections to nature for the sake of a higher reality pits us against our very life sources which we pillage, pollute, and destroy.

The feminist challenge to patriarchy strikes at the core of these destructive urges. The social, economic, political, and ideological maintenance of military institutions is a major characteristic of patriarchy. The ideologies and structures of gender difference, including the subordination of women, support the unilateral and hierarchical powers of male dominance and the need for supremacy. The transformation of patriarchy will not only liberate women. It is crucial to the survival of our planet. The creation of a nonpatriarchal theology is a crucial element in that survival.

To continue to rely on unilateral power for protection will not see us out of our morass. But to trust in heart, in erotic power, is a dangerous act. To challenge the powers of exploitation and destruction with love, care, and compassion is an act of monumental courage. Traveling with heart is fraught with difficulties. To face our own brokenheartedness and to touch the depths of our fears and pains can feel like a lonely journey into death. Our dangerous memories are frightening. Yet they have the power to transform. If our species, our very planet is to survive, we must take heart. And our theologies must help us find it.

Nothing else but our inborn need for self-love and for intimacy with others can sustain us and every other living thing on our planet. There, in our heartfelt connections we find the sacred mystery that births us all in a cosmic dance of erotic power.

Evocations of an honest, healing memory that returns us to heart can happen in unexpected places. The journey into the territories of erotic power like the women's journey to Jesus' tomb is a journey with surprises and no definite goals. It can only be followed as our hearts lead us. It is like Nelle Morton's description of the journey of a metaphor: trying to control it toward a predetermined outcome thwarts the process. The mystery of the journey's way stations and the unexpected twists and turns that startle, frighten, inspire, enliven, and heal us are the gifts of its grace. Those gifts are always available, even when we do not expect them. The fundamental question for our civilization and for all life as we know it on our planet is will we have the courage to give ourselves to the call of that mystery, to the active, forbearing, passionate gentleness that will not let life go.

Christa/Community is found in unexpected and expected places. Vast as the ocean, that community stretches far into the unexplored territories of erotic power. It is alive in the daily actions of those who, in small acts and large ones, live with courage, with heart.

We stand as witnesses against those who seek to dominate others and objectify and disconnect life. We also stand as witnesses against all theologies that continue to affirm divine power as paternalism and dominance. Erotic power is the only life-giving power. Our ability to live in its grace and to risk acting to stop the forces that crush it is what continually creates salvific acts. Spirit-Sophia and humanity as Christa/Community journey together into the territories of erotic power where we discover our love for the whole and compassionate being, the incarnation of divine love.

Notes

For complete information on works where only the title is given, see the Bibliography.

Introduction

1. Mary Potter Engel, in "A Weave of Women: Emerging Communities of the Feminist Reformation," Hoover Lecture, University of Chicago Divinity School, 23 April 1987, suggested that the twentieth century has witnessed the greatest reformation of the church and the greatest challenge to its self-identity since the sixteenth century.

2. Susan Griffin, in *Pornography and Silence: Culture's Revenge Against Nature*, pp. 82–154, discusses the metaphor of heart as the center of the self's yearning for Eros. The *Oxford English Dictionary* contains an extensive definition of shades of meaning for heart. Any number of dictionary definitions for heart list physical, emotional, and spiritual meanings for the word. The complex Hebrew meanings of the word *daath*, often translated as "to know" (both spiritually and carnally), approximate the nondualistic ways in which I use heart.

3. See the section on Asian women theologians in the *Journal of Feminist Studies in Religion* 3 (Fall 1987): 103–50; John Cobb, *Beyond Dialogue: Toward a Mutual Transformation of Christianity and Buddhism* (Philadelphia: Fortress Press, 1982), on interfaith dialogue, and *Christ in a Pluralistic Age* (Philadelphia: Westminster Press, 1975), on hope. Also Fred Eppsteiner and Dennis Maloney, *The Path of Compassion: Contemporary Writings on Engaged Buddhism* (Berkeley: Buddhist Peace Fellowship, 1985); Joanna Rogers Macy, *Despair and Personal Power in the Nuclear Age* (Philadelphia: New Society Publishers, 1983); and Jay B. McDaniel, "The God of the

Oppressed and the God Who Is Empty," in *God and Global Justice: Religion and Poverty in an Unequal World*, ed. Frederick Ferré and Rita H. Mataragnon (New York: Paragon House, 1985).

4. The question of the invisibility in feminism of black women's concerns is raised in Bell Hooks, *Ain't I a Woman: Black Women and Feminism* (Boston: South End Press, 1981); Gloria T. Hull, Patricia Bell Scott, and Barbara Smith, eds., *But Some of Us Are Brave* (Old Westbury, NY: Feminist Press, 1982); and the Mudflower Collective, *God's Fierce Whimsy: Christian Feminism and Theological Education* (New York: Pilgrim Press, 1985). Although she does not address Christianity, Audre Lorde raises a concern about the implicit racism in radical feminism in "An Open Letter to Mary Daly," in *Sister Outsider*. The sexism in black Christianity is addressed in Gayraud S. Wilmore and James H. Cone, *Black Theology: A Documentary History, 1966–1979* (Maryknoll, NY: Orbis, 1979), pp. 363–442, and an essay by Jacqueline Grant in Hull et al. For Asian perspectives, see the Asian women's essays cited in 3 above. For Latin America, see the essay by Pauline Turner in Yvonne Y. Haddad and Ellison B. Findly, eds., *Women, Religion, and Social Change* (Albany, NY: State University of New York Press, 1985), pp. 321–49.

*Chapter 1/The Character of Being Human
and the Making of Human Character*

1. Joanna Rogers Macy, in *Despair and Personal Power in the Nuclear Age* (New Haven: New Society Publishers, 1983), discusses Robert J. Lifton's concept of "psychic numbing" and the many factors that contribute to the denial of pain and suffering. "The great pivotal questions of life require us to stand before them in humility—at least for a moment, naked of know-how and shorn of self-assurance. Yet wanting to believe in our own power and savvy, we shy from what appears, even temporarily, to threaten them" (p. 12). Macy attributes despair to the repression of pain. The private experience of pain without a meaningful structure of understanding or sense of connection to others who care leads to despair. See, for example, the description of attempted suicide in Wendy Law Yone's *The Coffin Tree* (New York: Alfred A. Knopf, 1983).

2. Gerda Lerner, *The Creation of Patriarchy* (New York: Oxford University Press, 1986), p. 230.

3. See Richard J. Gelles and Claire Pedrick Cornell, *Intimate Violence in Families* (Beverly Hills: Sage, 1985), who address the extent of physical violence in American families and conclude love is in short supply. Adrienne Rich has written extensively on motherhood and the ambivalence behind nostalgic images of the family home. Florence Rush and Alice Miller also discuss the ideology of Western child abuse and the pervasiveness of its actuality. See Rich, *Of Woman Born* (New York: W. W. Norton, 1976); Rush, *The Best Kept Secret* (San Francisco: McGraw-Hill, 1980); and Miller, *The Drama of the Gifted Child: How Narcissistic Parents Form and Deform the*

Emotional Lives of Their Talented Children (New York: Basic Books, 1981), *For Your Own Good: Hidden Cruelty in Child-Rearing and the Roots of Violence* (New York: Farrar, Straus & Giroux, 1984), and *Thou Shalt Not Be Aware: Society's Betrayal of the Child* (New York: Farrar, Straus & Giroux, 1984).

4. Even when abuse in the home is acknowledged, theologians have sought to protect the ideology of the patriarchal family as divinely ordained. See, for example, Mary Potter's analysis of Calvin in "Gender Equality and Gender Hierarchy in Calvin's Theology," *Signs* 11, 4 (Summer 1986): 725–39; Joan Arnold's analysis of Barth in "Karl Barth's Theology of the Word of God: Or, How to Keep Women Silent and in Their Place," in *Women and Religion*, ed. Judith Plaskow and Joan Arnold (Missoula, MT: Scholars Press, 1974); or Rush's discussion in *The Best Kept Secret*, chap. 3.

5. Charlotte O'Kelly and Larry Carney, in *Women and Men in Society* (Belmont, CA: Wadsworth, 1986), Lerner, in *The Creation of Patriarchy*, and Peggy Reeves Sanday, in *Female Power and Male Dominance: On the Origins of Sexual Inequality*, discuss the relationship between social structures and religious ideas. Feminist theorists such as Barbara Deming and Zillah Eisenstein have revised Marxist theory using the feminist model of the control of reproduction. Hester Eisenstein, in *Contemporary Feminist Thought* (Boston: G. K. Hall, 1983) surveys various feminist approaches to the question of the biological origins of patriarchy.

6. The Western intellectual tradition has assumed notions of rational objectivity that belie the vested interests involved in any system of ideas. Alfred North White-head, in *Modes of Thought* (New York: Macmillan, 1938), criticizes this view of objectivity and asserts that interest is the underlying basis for thinking. Hence ideas have emotional roots. In fact, I would assert that rational concepts are often rationalizations for vested emotional interests such as racism, homophobia, and sexism, in which so-called objective science is used to prove prejudice. Susan Miller Okin analyzes such bias in political systems in *Women in Western Political Thought* (Princeton: Princeton University Press, 1979). I believe that the full understanding of ideas involves seeing their social and cultural roots and their psychological appeal, as well as their internal coherence.

7. Rosemary Radford Ruether, *Sexism and God-Talk*, p. 178.

8. The behavior of men in patriarchal Christianity, including violence, hierar-chical and anticommunitarian bias, misogyny, and exclusivist, defensive, in-group thinking, also indicates a lack of self-acceptance and inner peace. See Rosemary Radford Ruether's discussion of this in *Sexism and God-Talk*.

9. Robert McAfee Brown, in *Theology in a New Key* (Philadelphia: Westminster, 1978), explains the impact of liberation theology on American Christianity, as does Rosemary Radford Ruether, in *Liberation Theology: Human Hope Confronts Christian History and American Power* (New York: Paulist Press, 1972). Susan Brooks Thistle-thwaite, in *Metaphors for the Contemporary Church* (New York: Pilgrim Press, 1983), discusses ecclesiology in light of feminist and liberation challenges to the church.

10. For a brief summary description of object-relations theory, see Andrew H. Schauer, "Object Relations Theory: A Dialogue with Donald B. Kinsley, "*Journal of Counseling and Development* 65 (September 1986): 35–39.

11. This summary of Miller is based on her books published before 1985. Miller uses the Freudian term which applies approximately to the first two years of life. Various theorists use different names for the stages involved. Perhaps because of the absence of an overt discussion of gender issues in her work, Miller has not, until recently, been classified as a feminist theorist. However, I include her here because she has aligned herself with work done by Susan Griffin and Florence Rush and because her work both substantiates and supplements other work in feminist psy- chology. See Miller's afterward to the American edition of *Thou Shalt Not be Aware*, in which she cites Griffin and Rush. Other feminists who use object-relations theory include Nancy Chodorow, Carol Gilligan, Naomi Goldenberg, Luise Eichenbaum, Catherine Keller, and Susie Orbach.

12. See Beverly Harrison's *Making the Connections: Essays in Feminist Social Ethics* (Boston: Beacon, 1985) and Ruether's *Sexism and God-Talk* for a discussion of the importance of anger that empowers feminist consciousness. Barbara Deming, in *We Are All Part of One Another*, pp. 206–17, discusses the importance of anger as crucial to pacifism. "I suggest that if we are willing to confront our own most seemingly personal angers, in their raw state, and take upon ourselves the task of translating this raw anger into the disciplined anger of the search for change, we will find ourselves in a position to speak more persuasively to comrades about the need to root out from all anger the spirit of murder" (p. 217). For a somewhat more negative, Freudian object-relations view of anger, see Naomi Goldenberg's analysis of Melanie Klein in "Anger in the Body," *Journal of Feminist Studies in Religion* 2 (Fall 1986:) 36–50. Using the idea of aggression, Klein developed the theory that guilt was the key motive behind the need to care for others. Goldenberg argues, and I agree, that we need to learn better ways to integrate anger and aggression into relationships of affection.

Chapter 2/The Heart of Erotic Power:
The Incarnation of Divine Love

1. Haunani-Kay Trask, *Eros and Power: The Promise of Feminist Theory* (Philadel- phia: University of Pennsylvania Press, 1986), pp. 92–93. Trask summarizes Eros and power in feminist theory. She surveys writers such as Daly and Rich who implicitly use a concept of Eros in their work and those such as Griffin and Lorde who specifically identify Eros or the erotic as one form of power. As I will argue, I believe Eros as power has a sacred dimension that leads us to an understanding of incarnate Spirit.

Trask contrasts Eros with logos, using Marcuse's analysis of narcissism, which understands Freud's death instinct as the urge to relieve the tensions of struggling against repression and suffering.

2. Loomer's essay is found in *Process Studies* 6 (Spring 1976): 5–32.

3. Harriett Lerner, in *The Dance of Anger: A Woman's Guide to Changing the Patterns of Intimate Relationships* (New York: Harper & Row, 1985), explains the misconceptions involved in thinking of feelings as directly caused by others' behaviors. She suggests that events trigger reactions, thereby providing the necessary stimulus for further events. However, the particular shape of further events is determined largely by the past history, memories, and inner feelings of the participants. Hence a variety of actions, as self chosen, are possible to any event.

4. Alice Miller, *For Your Own Good: Hidden Cruelty in Child-Rearing and the Roots of Violence* (New York: Farrar, Straus & Giroux, 1984), pp. 84–85.

5. Carol Kuhn, in a lecture at a conference on "Women in Mental Health," 10 October 1986, in Kansas City, MO, made a helpful distinction between the two in her discussion of anger and learned helplessness.

6. Donald W. Winnicott, *Playing and Reality* (New York: Basic Books, 1971).

7. Charles Hartshorne, *The Logic of Perfection* (La Salle, IL: Open Court, 1962), p. 230.

8. In Audre Lorde, *Sister Outsider.*

9. In *Signs* 7, 3 (Spring 1982): 641–60.

10. In *Journal of Feminist Studies in Religion* 2 (Fall 1986): 23–38.

11. See Marjorie Shostak, *Nisa: The Life and Words of a !Kung Woman*, and Richard Katz, *Boiling Energy: Community Healing among the Kalahari Kung* (Cambridge: Harvard University Press, 1984).

12. Werner H. Kelber, *The Oral and Written Gospel: The Hermeneutics of Speaking and Writing in the Synoptic Tradition, Mark, Paul and Q* (Philadelphia: Fortress Press, 1983).

13. Charles Hartshorne, *Omnipotence and Other Theological Mistakes* (Albany, NY: State University of New York Press, 1984).

14. Alfred North Whitehead, *Adventures of Ideas* (New York: Free Press, 1967).

15. Bernard Meland, *Fallible Forms and Symbols* (Philadelphia: Fortress Press, 1976).

16. Henry Nelson Wieman, *The Source of Human Good* (Carbondale, IL: Southern Illinois University Press, 1967).

Chapter 3/The Feminist Redemption of Christ

1. Alfred North Whitehead, *Modes of Thought* (New York: Macmillan, 1938).

2. As I recall, the first use of the term Christa was in reference to the crucifix in the Cathedral of Saint John the Divine in New York City. The Christ on the crucifix, labeled Christa, was female. In using Christa instead of Christ, I am using a term that points away from a sole identification of Christ with Jesus. In combining it with community, I want to shift the focus of salvation away from heroic individuals, male or female. I agree with Nelle Morton, in *The Journey Is Home* (Boston: Beacon Press, 1985), pp. 194–98, that new realities must be accompanied by

metaphors that shatter old, conventional ways of thinking and usher in new images. Using the term Christa/Community affirms my conviction about the sacredness of community.

3. J. F. Bethune-Baker, *An Introduction to the Early History of Christian Doctrine: To the Time of the Council of Chalcedon*, 8th ed. (London, Methuen, 1949).

4. Aloys Grillmeier, in *Christ in Christian Tradition* (Atlanta, GA: John Knox Press, 1975), pp. 3–105, summarizes the diversity of biblical christologies: "Within the limits marked out on the one hand by the synoptists and on the other by John and Paul, the christology of the New Testament itself already displays considerable diversity. We have, for example, the contrast between a messianic christology (the Acts speeches, the synoptic gospels) and the Johannine idea of the Logos; the factors which determine a portrayal of Christ may be salvation history (synoptics; Rom.; Gal.), cosmology (Eph.; Col. I, 15ff), liturgy (Heb.) or apocalyptic (Rev.). The picture of Christ given by the New Testament already shows sometimes predominantly Judaistic, elsewhere predominantly Hellenistic features" (p. 33). For a discussion of the formation of the Chalcedonian creed, including the varieties of earlier heresies, see Grillmeier and Bethune-Baker, *An Introduction to the Early History of Christian Doctrine*.

5. Schubert Ogden, *The Point of Christology* (New York: Harper & Row, 1982); Alfred North Whitehead, *Science and the Modern Mind* (New York: Macmillan, 1925).

6. Tom Driver, *Christ in a Changing World: Toward an Ethical Christology* (New York: Crossroad, 1981).

7. William Beardslee, *A House for Hope: A Study in Process and Biblical Thought* (Philadelphia: Westminster Press, 1972), p. 100.

Chapter 4/The Gospel of Mark: Erotic Power at Work

1. Elisabeth Schüssler Fiorenza, *In Memory of Her*, p. 318.

2. Werner H. Kelber, *The Oral and Written Gospel: The Hermeneutics of Speaking and Writing in the Synoptic Tradition, Mark, Paul, and Q* (Philadelphia: Fortress Press, 1983).

3. In *Semeia* 11 (1978): 83–112.

4. Gert Theissen, *The Miracle Stories of the Early Christian Tradition* (Philadelphia: Fortress Press, 1983).

5. Klaus Seybold and Ulrich B. Mueller, *Sickness and Healing* (Nashville, TN: Abingdon Press, 1981), p. 131.

6. In chapter 4 of *In Memory of Her*, Schüssler Fiorenza discusses this story at length. Her discussion is summarized here.

7. I am grateful to Dr. Carole Myscofski, Dept. of Religious Studies, University of Missouri, Columbia, MO, for help with the Greek in these texts.

8. In *In Memory of Her* Schüssler Fiorenza speaks of the Spirit which empowers the "*ekklēsia* of women" because the civil-political use of *ekklēsia* in the New Testament

implies an assembly of free citizens who gather to decide their own spiritual-political affairs, something women have been denied access to. "The gospel is not a matter of the individual soul; it is the communal proclamation of the life-giving power of Spirit-Sophia and of God's vision of an alternative community and world. . . . The focal point of early Christian self-understanding was not a holy book or a cultic rite, not mystic experience and magic invocation, but a set of relationships: the experience of God's presence among one another and through one another" (pp. 344–45). While our positions are not that different, I prefer to use the term Christa/Community to identify those empowered by the Spirit-Sophia of erotic power who live by heart which distinguishes it from church. Church is one, but not the only manifestation of Christa/Community.

Chapter 5/The Gospel of Mark:
Erotic Power in the Shadows

1. Henry Nelson Wieman, *The Source of Human Good* (Carbondale, IL: Southern Illinois University Press, 1967), p. 43.

2. Clark Williamson, *Has God Rejected His People?* (Nashville, TN: Abingdon Press, 1980).

3. Klaus Seybold and Ulrich B. Mueller, in *Sickness and Healing* (Nashville, TN: Abingdon Press, 1981), pp. 154–55, discuss the use of oils as unguents.

4. In Morton, *The Journey Is Home* (Boston: Beacon Press, 1985).

5. In *In Memory of Her* Schüssler Fiorenza makes a strong statement about the primacy of the female disciples during the passion narrative.

> It is a woman who recognizes Jesus' suffering messiahship and, in a prophetic-sign action, anoints Jesus for his burial, while "some" of the disciples reprimand her. Further, it is a servant woman who challenges Peter to act on his promise not to betray Jesus. In doing so she unmasks and exposes him for what he is, a betrayer. Finally two women, Mary of Magdala and Mary (the mother) of Joses, witness the place where Jesus is buried (15:47), and three women receive the news of his resurrection (16:1–8). Thus at the end of Mark's Gospel the women disciples emerge as examples of suffering discipleship and true leadership. They are the apostolic eye-witnesses of Jesus' death, burial, and resurrection. . . . Wherever the gospel is preached and heard, promulgated and read, what the women have done is not totally forgotten because the Gospel story remembers that the discipleship and apostolic leadership of women are integral parts of Jesus' "alternative" praxis of agape and service. [pp. 321, 334]

Bibliography

The following bibliography of works not cited in full in the text is provided especially for those interested in the research in feminist theory that is the background for this work. The explosion in feminist theory since 1975 represented in this bibliography will be of interest to readers whose formal education was prior to the transformative impact of women's studies on academic disciplines, especially in theology.

Anzualda, Gloria and Cherrie Moraga, eds. *This Bridge Called My Back: Writings by Radical Women of Color*. Watertown, MA: Persephone Press, 1981.

Basow, Susan. *Gender Stereotypes: Traditions and Alternatives*. Belmont, CA: Brooks/ Cole Publishing Co., 1986.

Brooten, Bernadette. "Feminist Perspectives on New Testament Exegesis." *Concilium: Religion in the Eighties*. Ed. Hans Küng and Jürgen Moltmann. New York: Seabury Press, 1980.

Brownmiller, Susan. *Against Our Will: Men, Women and Rape*. New York: Simon and Schuster, 1975.

Chesler, Phyllis. *Women and Madness*. New York: Doubleday, 1972.

Christ, Carol. *Diving Deep and Surfacing: Women Writers on Spiritual Quest*. Boston: Beacon Press, 1980.

————and Judith Plaskow. *Womanspirit Rising*. New York: Harper & Row, 1979.

Christian, Barbara. *Black Feminist Criticism: Perspectives on Black Women Writers*. New York: Pergamon Press, 1985.

Chodorow, Nancy. *The Reproduction of Mothering: Psychoanalysis and the Sociology of Gender*. Los Angeles: University of California Press, 1978.

Cooey, Paula. "The Power of Transformation and the Transformation of Power." *Journal of Feminist Studies in Religion* 1 (Spring 1985): 23–36.

Daly, Mary. *Beyond God the Father: Toward a Philosophy of Women's Liberation*. Boston: Beacon Press, 1973.

————. *Gyn/Ecology: The Metaethics of Radical Feminism*. Boston: Beacon Press, 1978.

Davaney, Sheila Greeve, ed. *Feminism and Process Thought*. New York: Edwin Mellen Press, 1981.

116

Davis, Angela Yvonne. *Women, Race, and Class.* New York: Random House, 1981.

Deming, Barbara. *We Are All Part of One Another: A Barbara Deming Reader.* Ed. Jane Meyerding. New Haven: New Society Publishers, 1984.

Dinnerstein, Dorothy. *The Mermaid and the Minotaur: Sexual Arrangements and Human Malaise.* New York: Harper & Row, 1976.

Dunfee, Susan. "Christianity and the Liberation of Women." Ph.D. diss., Claremont Graduate School, 1985.

Ehrenreich, Barbara. *The Hearts of Men: American Dreams and the Flight from Commitment.* Garden City, NY: Anchor Press/Doubleday, 1984.

——— and Deidre English. *Complaints and Disorders: the Sexual Politics of Sickness.* Old Westbury, NY: Feminist Press, 1973.

——— and Deidre English. *Witches, Midwives, and Nurses: A History of Women Healers.* Old Westbury, NY: Feminist Press, 1973.

Eichenbaum, Luise and Susie Orbach. *Understanding Women: A Feminist Psychoanalytic Approach.* New York: Basic Books, 1983.

Eisenstein, Zillah. *The Radical Future of Liberal Feminism.* New York: Longman Press, 1981.

Falk, Marcia. "Notes on Composing New Blessings: Toward a Feminist Jewish Reconstruction of Prayer." *Journal of Feminist Studies in Religion* 3 (Spring 1987): 39–53.

Fiorenza, Elisabeth Schüssler, *In Memory of Her: A Feminist Theological Reconstruction of Christian Origins.* New York: Crossroad Publishing Co., 1983.

Fischer, Clare Benedicks, Betsy Brenneman, and Anne McGrew Bennett, eds. *Women in a Strange Land: Search for a New Image.* Philadelphia: Fortress Press, 1975.

French, Marilyn. *Beyond Power: On Women, Men, and Morals.* New York: Summit Books, 1985.

Giddings, Paula. *When and Where I Enter: The Impact of Black Women on Race and Sex in America.* New York: Bantam Books, 1984.

Gilligan, Carol. *In a Different Voice: Psychological Theory and Women's Development.* Cambridge: Harvard University Press, 1982.

Goldenberg, Naomi. "Anger in the Body: Feminism, Religion and Kleinian Psychoanalytic Theory." *Journal of Feminist Studies in Religion* 2 (Fall 1986): 39–50.

———. "Archetypal Theory and the Separation of Mind and Body—Reason Enough to Turn to Freud?" *Journal of Feminist Studies in Religion* 1 (Spring 1985): 55–72.

———. *Changing of the Gods: Feminism and the End of Traditional Religions.* Boston: Beacon Press, 1979.

Goldstein, Valerie Saiving. "The Human Situation: A Feminine View." *Journal of Religion* 40 (April 1960): 100–112.

Grahn, Judy. *Descent to the Roses of the Family.* Iowa City: Common Lives/Lesbian Lives, 1986.

Griffin, Susan. *Pornography and Silence: Culture's Revenge Against Nature*. New York: Harper & Row, 1981.

———. "The Way of All Ideology." *Signs* 7, no.3 (Spring 1982): 641–60.

———. *Woman and Nature: the Roaring Inside Her*. New York: Harper & Row, 1979.

Herman, Judith L. *Father-Daughter Incest*. Cambridge: Harvard University Press, 1981.

Heschel, Susanna. *On Being a Jewish Feminist: A Reader*. New York: Schocken Books, 1983.

Heyward, Carter. "Heterosexist Theology: Being Above It All." *Journal of Feminist Studies in Religion* 3 (Spring 1987): 29–38.

———. *The Redemption of God: A Theology of Mutual Relation*. Ann Arbor, MI: University Microfilms International, 1979.

———. "An Unfinished Symphony of Liberation: The Radicalization of Christian Feminism Among White U.S. Women." *Journal of Feminist Studies in Religion* 1 (Spring 1985): 99–118.

Janeway, Elizabeth. *Powers of the Weak*. New York: Alfred A. Knopf, 1980.

Kalven, Janet and Mary I. Buckley, eds. *Women's Spirit Bonding*. New York: Pilgrim Press, 1984.

Keller, Catherine. *From a Broken Web: Separation, Sexism, and Self*. Boston: Beacon Press, 1986.

Langland, Elizabeth and Walter Gove, eds. *A Feminist Perspective in the Academy*. Chicago: University of Chicago Press, 1981.

Lerner, Harriett Goldhor. "Internal Prohibitions Against Female Anger." *American Journal of Psychoanalysis* 40, no. 2 (1980): 137–48.

Lips, Hilary M. *Women, Men, and the Psychology of Power*. Englewood Cliffs, NJ: Prentice-Hall, 1981.

Lorde, Audre. *Sister Outsider*. Trumansberg, NY: Crossing Press, 1984.

Lott, Bernice. *Women's Lives: Themes and Variations in Gender Learning*. Monterey, CA: Brooks/Cole, 1987.

Maccoby, Eleanor E. ed. *The Development of Sex Differences*. Palo Alto, CA: Stanford University Press, 1976.

Malbon, Elizabeth Struthers. "Fallible Followers: Women and Men in the Gospel of Mark." *Semeia* 28 (1983): 29–48.

———. *Narrative Space and Mythic Meaning in Mark*. San Francisco: Harper & Row, 1986.

McAllister, Pam, ed. *Reweaving the Web of Life: Feminism and Nonviolence*. Philadelphia: New Society Publishers, 1982.

Miller, Jean Baker. *Toward a New Psychology of Women*. Boston: Beacon Press, 1976.

Ochs, Carol. *The Myth Behind the Sex of God*. Boston: Beacon Press, 1977.

Olsen, Tillie. *Silences*. New York: Delta/Seymour Lawrence, 1979.

Pagels, Elaine H. *The Gnostic Gospels: A New Account of the Origins of Christianity*. New York: Random House, 1979.

Plaskow, Judith. *Sex, Sin and Grace: Women's Experiences and the Theologies of Reinhold Niebuhr and Paul Tillich.* Washington, DC: University of America Press, 1980.

Reardon, Betty A. *Sexism and the War System.* New York: Teachers College Press, 1985.

Rich, Adrienne. *The Dream of a Common Language: Poems 1974–1977.* New York: W. W. Norton, 1978.

————. *The Fact of a Door Frame: Poems Selected and New 1950–1984.* New York: Norton, 1984.

————. *On Lies, Secrets, and Silence: Selected Prose 1966–1978.* New York: W. W. Norton, 1979.

————. *A Wild Patience Has Taken Me This Far: Poems 1978–1981.* New York: W. W. Norton, 1981.

Rigney, Barbara Hill. *Madness and Sexual Politics in the Feminist Novel: Studies in Bronte, Woolf, Lessing and Atwood.* Madison: University of Wisconsin Press, 1978.

Ruether, Rosemary Radford. *Disputed Questions on Being a Christian.* Nashville, TN: Abingdon Press, 1982.

————. *New Woman/New Earth: Sexist Ideologies and Human Liberation.* New York: Seabury Press, 1975.

————. *Sexism and God-Talk: Toward a Feminist Theology.* Boston: Beacon Press, 1983.

————. *To Change the World: Christology and Cultural Criticism.* New York: Crossroad Publishing Co., 1981.

———— and Eleanor McLaughlin. *Women of Spirit: Female Leadership in the Jewish and Christian Traditions.* New York: Simon and Schuster, 1979.

———— and Rosemary S. Keller, eds. *Women and Religion in America: Vol. 1, The Nineteenth Century, A Documentary History.* San Francisco: Harper & Row, 1981.

Russell, Diana and Nicole Van de Ven, eds. *Crimes Against Women: Proceedings of the International Tribunal.* Millbrae, CA: Les Femmes, 1976.

———— and Nancy Howell. "The Prevalence of Rape in the United States Revisited." *Signs* 8, no. 4 (1983): 688–95.

Russell, Letty M., ed. *Feminist Interpretations of the Bible.* Philadelphia: Westminster Press, 1985.

————. *Human Liberation in a Feminist Perspective.* Philadelphia: Westminster Press, 1974.

Saiving, Valerie (see Goldstein, Valerie Saiving).

Sanday, Peggy Reeves. *Female Power and Male Dominance: On the Origins of Sexual Inequality.* Cambridge: Cambridge University Press, 1981.

Schaef, Anne Wilson. *Women's Reality: An Emerging Female System in the White Male Society.* Minneapolis, MN: Winston Press, 1981.

Shostak, Marjorie. *Nisa: The Life and Words of a !Kung Woman.* New York: Vintage Books, 1983.

Spretnak, Charlene, ed. *The Politics of Women's Spirituality*. Garden City, NY: Anchor Press/Doubleday, 1982.

Starhawk. *Dreaming the Dark: Magic, Sex, and Politics*. Boston: Beacon Press, 1982.

————. *The Spiral Dance: A Rebirth of the Ancient Religion of the Great Goddess*. New York: Harper & Row, 1979.

Stone, Merlin. *Ancient Mirrors of Womanhood*. 2 vols. New York: New Sibylline Books, 1979.

————. *When God Was a Woman*. New York: Dial Press, 1976.

Tennis, Diane. "Reflections on the Maleness of Jesus." *Cross Currents* (Summer 1978).

Tetlow, Elisabeth M. *Women and Ministry in the New Testament*. New York: Paulist Press, 1980.

Trible, Phyllis. *God and the Rhetoric of Sexuality*. Philadelphia: Fortress Press, 1978.

————. *Texts of Terror: Literary-Feminist Readings of Biblical Narratives*. Philadelphia: Fortress Press, 1984.

Wahlberg, Rachel Conrad. *Jesus According to a Woman*. New York: Paulist Press, 1975.

Weidman, Judith L., ed. *Christian Feminism: Visions of a New Humanity*. San Francisco: Harper & Row, 1984.

Wilson-Kastner, Patricia. *Faith, Feminism, and the Christ*. Philadelphia: Fortress Press, 1983.

Woolf, Virginia. *A Room of One's Own*. New York: Harcourt, Brace, Jovanovich, 1973.

————. *Three Guineas*. New York: Harcourt, Brace, Jovanovich, 1963.

Index

Abuse: of children, 12–14, 17–19, 110n–11n; of the body, 21–22, 26; in theological images, 50, 53–57. *See also* Children; Women

Achievement, 11–12, 14–15, 27–28

Agape, 40, 53, 70, 115n

Aggression, 25–27, 112n

Agrarian societies, 44

Alienation, alienating, alienated, 6, 40–41, 47, 54, 59–61, 73

Anamnesis. See Memory

Androcentrism, androcentric, xii–xiii, 2, 5, 34–35, 51, 67. *See also* Misogyny; Patriarchy; Women: subordination

Androgyny, androgynous, xiii, 60–61, 63

Anger, fury, rage, xv, 10–11, 112n, 113n; in adults, 17–21, 23, 30, 32; in biblical texts, 78, 89; in liberation, 65–66

Apatheia, 49, 53

Apollinarianism, 57

Arianism, Arius, 57

Arnold, Joan, 111n

Asian, Asian American, Japanese, xv–xvii, 109n, 110n

Atonement, 55–58

Authority, authorities, 13–14, 32, 49, 55, 64, 68, 80, 85, 87–88. *See also* Power

Barth, Karl, 111n

Basileia, 58, 66, 69, 73, 76, 82, 85

Beardslee, William, 68, 114n

Bethune-Baker, J. F., 55, 114n

Bible, biblical, xiii, xvii, 4, 50, 58, 65, 67–69, 71, 74, 76, 114n

Birth, 6, 8–9, 17, 90

Black, xi, xv, xvii, 20, 110n

Blame. *See* Punishment

Body, bodies, 13, 21–22, 26, 37, 112n; embodied, embodiment, 41, 62; mind and body analogy, 46

Body, women's. *See* Women: subordination

Broken heart, brokenhearted, brokenheartedness: in biblical texts, 77, 80–82, 87–88; healing of, 25, 87–88; patriarchy, 41–42; self, 12–13, 16–17, 22, 32, 48; society, xi, 35, 49; in theology, xiii, 7, 51–53, 69, 76, 87–88; victims, 65, 74. *See also* Pain; Suffering

Brown, Robert McAfee, 111n

Buddhism, Buddhist, xv–xvi, 35, 109n

Calvin, John, 111n

Capitalism, 40, 74

Carney, Larry, 111n

121